How to conquer a mountain: Kilimanjaro lessons

Copyright © 2014 Sue and John R. Irving
All rights reserved.
No part of this book may be reproduced or transmitted in any form or by any means, electronic or mechanical, including photocopying, recording, or by any information storage and retrieval system without express written permission from the authors.

Cover designed by Sue Irving

ISBN: 978-1-502-71920-1

Table of Contents

Preface 1

Climbing Applications 2

Welcome Back to Africa 4

The Adventure Starts in Earnest 19

How to Eat an Elephant 36

Crossroads 48

Walls 72

Preparing for Summit Night 87

Dealing with What Is 98

Kilimanjaro Song 119

A Successful Shopping Expedition 130

Epilogue 131

Acknowledgements

Sue:
To climb a mountain like Kilimanjaro, you need experienced guides to show the way, reliable porters to help to carry your load and cheerleaders who chivvy you along when you are ready to give up. Neither our climb nor this book would have happened without the encouragement and support of many people.

A special thanks to those who trekked with us and made our experience so memorable (do not worry, fellow trekkers, your names have been changed!), the members of our monthly writers' group and to Crysse, Dinks, Richard, Michael, Gill, Martin, Loli and Dave for their feedback and proof-reading.

John:
I owe a special thanks to my brother-in-law Thomas who insisted that we bought a different kit.

I am aware that our mountain guides' knowledge and encouragement were vital, as were the porters' willingness to lug our tents, sleeping bags and sundries for the trip. Even though they are unlikely to read this book, I still want to say *asante sana* (thank you very much) to my African friends.

Preface

I have always been fascinated by the link between outer and inner journeys. I therefore suggested to John that we should each keep a travel journal of our Kilimanjaro trek to capture not just our physical, but also the emotional and spiritual journeys involved.

John and I see the world differently and have our own approach to things (as you will soon find out!), but we still had no idea how different our experiences would be.

We hope that our accounts will give future climbers a taste of what trekking is like. However, this book is as much about how to handle life with its valleys and mountain top experiences, as it is about two people's particular journeys at a particular point in time. It may therefore be of interest to those who have no inclination to ever set foot on any physical mountain, let alone a mountain the size of Kilimanjaro.

We dedicate this book to all those who dare to climb mountains and to those who have to climb mountains not of their choosing.

Sue Irving, November 2014

Climbing Applications

April 2012

Greetings Kilimanjaro,
My earliest memories are of you floating above the horizon, a white sash in a blue sky far away in the bush-covered distance, a sight that would only fade in the red African twilight. You stirred my imagination. What wonders lay beyond my boundaries?

And then the joy and excitement of finally exploring your mysteries before my world changed forever.

I still remember the sorrow and upheaval of leaving the land I knew for uncertainty and frequent changes of abode, my elderly parents' anxiety as I failed to shine in class and on field in England, and the realisation that there was no longer a place for me in East Africa when I visited in '73.

I have no desire to refresh fading memories, but have committed myself to climbing you again. Ready or not, here I come. *Harambee*!
John

Dear Kilimanjaro,
I am organised, determined and efficient - you know you can rely on us Germans to get things right. I am aiming to take photos that will show off your majesty to those who do not have the privilege of climbing you. As a life-long learner, I am looking forward to the lessons you are going to teach me on the way to the

summit. I will never be particularly sporty and courageous, but I will make up for it through preparation and diligence. I am not afraid of hard work.

I hope you consider me a worthy candidate for exploring your heights. Sorry that it took me so long to take you up on your invitation. To be honest, I need a project to focus on right now. I am not quite ready to grieve for what won't be.

Yours sincerely,
Sue

Welcome Back to Africa

February 2013. As we drive through the villages, African life passes by. We jolt through homesteads and past *dukas*. The general purpose shops nowadays display Vodafone top up signs. We hurtle past bikes, motorbikes, mango trees, and tethered goats. Tied-up *ghombis*, Africa's humped-back, long-horned cows, are also waiting to be milked. I watch the *daladalas*, the local version of a taxi, hoot and manoeuvre between overloaded buses and cars. There is purpose in the chaos. Most vehicles are moving luggage mountains. The red, pink, black and brown suitcases are streaked with red dust, which creates a lurid effect in the afternoon sun. I am back -no doubt about it...

I cannot remember when I have last slept so little, the curse of having been sandwiched in the middle seat during the overnight journey from London to Nairobi. I should have organised the flights myself. Then I would have had an aisle seat. I hope we are there soon...

I should have known that Sue meant what she said.

"I thought that Kilimanjaro would be a better choice. Hill walking in the Himalayas is too extravagant", Sue had announced. She had already checked the internet; there was one interesting trek coming up next February. I was stumped. First walking in Nepal and now climbing Kilimanjaro?

Sue has never been keen on mountains, so why this sudden interest? Not just any mountain, but one of the highest mountains in the world!

"Shall I go ahead and book the trip? You have always said that you want us to have a more active holiday!" Sue gave me a look that did not encourage disagreement, and I obliged.

"Yes, go ahead", I said.

I figured she deserved a treat after all she had been through. I was certain that she would not go through with this anyway, thinking back to her protests and the emotion stirred up when we climbed to the top of Lion's Head in South Africa. That mountain was nothing compared to Kili.

"I have been reading what climbers have said about training, so I have devised a training schedule to get fit," Sue announced shortly afterwards. O dear, this was ominous. My wife has the ability to get very involved in projects before they have even begun. I could tell that her teeth were in this already, and extracting them would be nearly impossible now. I did not even try. Will I be able to hack this though?

We finally pass the "Welcome to Arusha" sign and are soon disgorged at the Arusha Hotel. Smartly dressed and deferential employees pick up our luggage and carry it into the posh hallway. All I want right now is to jump into the outdoor swimming pool and let its warm water uncramp my body. And a cold beer would be good!

If its advertising is to be believed, the Arusha Hotel is nowadays frequented by Hollywood icons and US Presidents, but today the adrenaline-fuelled laughter of our group of would-be trekkers echoes through its entrance hall. Porters are carrying in our duffle bags and rucksacks and dump them on the polished marble floor, turning this haven of tranquillity into a youth hostel.

While John is jostling for our room key, I explore our surroundings. Hot air drifts in through the terrace door that leads into a garden where banana trees and tropical flowers are basking in the bright afternoon sun. I decline the garden's invitation to come and rest for a while and study the black and white photos in the entrance hall instead.

They show gentlemen and ladies in safari clothes posing in front of a grand building in the countryside. Were those people off lion hunting or conquering mountains? Their expressions do not tell. Back then, the British still knew how to keep a rein on their emotions. I imagine them speaking with well-modulated voices and behaving with a sense of decorum, but can they really blame us for breaking the unwritten rules?

I for one cannot wait to set foot on Kilimanjaro. I am the first to admit that I am not the intrepid explorer type, but Kilimanjaro has been calling me for the last decade.

How long does it take to get a key? My hiking boots feel like steel shackles. I wish I had not been swayed by my climbing-enthusiastic brother-in-law to replace the lightweight boots I had been training in for this sturdier pair. Trekkers say that every extra gram counts when you are climbing Kili.

I know that I am not in the best place to make judgment calls right now. I try to uncoil my spine by attempting a Pilates roll-down. My hands barely get beyond my knees, and I can hear my vertebrae clicking back into place when I roll up.

John finally motions that we are ready to go. There are already a handful of trekkers queuing for the small lift, so we decide to carry our bags upstairs - good practice for the days ahead. Our room is spacious and bright and contains two separate double beds protected by mosquito nets. If I cannot sleep properly tonight, there is no hope for me on the mountain! It is a pleasant surprise to spend the last night before the trek in style.

I am tempted to throw myself on the bed straight away, but there are so many things that need to be organised first. We are spending an additional week in Africa, so I need to sort out what can stay behind. I empty out all our bags and pockets to get an overview of what we have. Big mistake! The room seems to shrink and with it my energy reserves.

I remember Sue showing me page upon page downloaded from the internet, listing the recommended kit: weather proof jackets, liners, climbing pants, gloves - the clothing lists went on and on. And then there was another list with the right "eaties" - nuts, dried fruit and energy bars. Sue had to get it all of course, and the "fruit" of her labour is all around us now. Time to make a swift exit...

I am standing in the middle of the room, paralysed by the chaos, when there is a knock at the door.

"Sundown service", the maid announces as she carefully steps over the piles of clothing on the floor.

She closes the curtains and looks questioningly at the beds, which have disappeared under yet more stuff. I must look like a colonial invader to her. I tell the maid that she does not need to worry about the beds, and she leaves without making any attempt to fluff up our pillows for the night.

Sue wants the kettle boiled. Not a problem you would think, but this is Africa. I notice a two point European plug falling out of a British square pin socket. I pick up the plug and examine it more closely. The round pins have been hammered into shape to fit the socket.

Sue is not happy with this display of local ingenuity, and I walk down to reception where an old man gives me a look of amused contempt when I explain our problem. He says he will send someone up, so I leave the kettle with him.

Lo and behold, a room service girl comes to the room with the same kettle. She manages to wedge the plug into the socket, using a spoon to open the earth pin. Luckily Sue is too occupied with other things to watch the procedure. Her world is whole again for the time being.

I make another attempt at packing, picking up first this item then that, unsure what to do with either of them. The East Africans would probably say that I am behaving like a typical *mzungu*. This apparently not only means white person in Swahili, but someone who is walking around aimlessly. For some reason I cannot close my duffle bag, even though I have already decanted post-trekking items into the big white plastic sacks that the hotel has provided. I have to call John over to help me close the zip.

John says that I have brought far too much stuff. It is easy for him to talk. My bag was already three-quarters full before I packed clothes, toiletries, snacks and other useful items: There is the down sleeping-bag I hired, which takes up half my duffle-bag. Then there is the Thermarest mattress, which I foolishly tried out at home. I wanted to see how the self-inflation mechanism works. Unfortunately, I have never managed to deflate it completely. I also have to take a lot of sanitary items, just in case things get out of control again. The doctors keep reassuring me that they won't, but they have been wrong so far.

"We will get fed, you know!" John grumbles. He is eying my collection of wine gums, energy bars, dried fruits and flapjacks. All my guidebooks have said that it is important to take snacks you really like. It is apparently hard to keep eating at altitude, and I have no intention of being turned back because I have run out of energy.

I am particularly pleased with my homemade flapjacks, which combine ingredients that provide iron, balance hormones and increase energy without leading to wild swings in blood sugar levels. Friends and family eyed my concoction with suspicion at first, as molasses and spirulina give the flapjacks an unexpected (OK, unappealing) colour - but most are now converts. John is always looking forward to the flapjacks as a special treat, but if he does not stop moaning, he won't get any!

Shall I take my Kindle or the inspiring paperback about life lessons learned whilst walking the Camino? They are not that heavy, so I decide to take both. I also pack enough wool to knit a scarf. Maybe it is a bit of an overkill, but how can I know in advance what will help me unwind after a hard day's climb? Knitting may help to calm my pre-summit nerves.

With a lot of pushing, punching and squeezing, John and I finally manage to close the zip of my duffle-bag. I hope the zip is sturdier than it looks. It is probably best to open this bag as little as possible - preferably not before we reach our first overnight camp.

The afternoon heat is still stifling, and I am looking forward to an acclimatizing and cooling swim to rid myself of the flight stress. Instead, I have to sit through the pre-climb meeting. I am not a "meeting and greeting" kind of person, but I can see the need.

We assemble in a room that looks like a typical assembly hall cum gym in any English school - including the plastic chairs that have been stacked on the side. More and more would-be climbers drift in, but forty minutes after the announced time, we finally start.

Our Action Challenge leader Steward introduces us to Summits Africa, the local company which will provide our guides and porters. Their boss is all "rep" - he reminds us of the dangers of altitude, to take the tablets which help us to adjust to the changing height and also Malaria tablets, even though there are no mosquitoes once we are above forest height. Then there is the spiel about the need to drink plenty of water and wear sun protection. Summits Africa also have rules about not walking around unsupervised, keeping to the paths at all times, no alcohol and the right to terminate anybody's climb if they are unhappy with a person's conduct.

"It is our aim that everybody will walk all the way down the mountain, regardless of how far up they get", we are told almost as soon as the local director has introduced himself. I do not like the reminder that it is unlikely that all of us will get to the summit.

Action Challenge have a success rate of 90%+, which is higher than the average, but this is still no consolation for the people who do not make it. The unlucky 10% have become more real since I received an e-mail from a climber I met on my training walk in January. She had to leave the mountain on day 3 because of pneumonia. She was gutted, she said. I can imagine. After all her training and preparation she did not even make it to summit day - I would not be able to cope with the disappointment.

Kilimanjaro was first calling me ten years ago when a young woman came to see me to deal with her father's suicide. For months we scrambled through the treacherous, slippery terrain of her unprocessed grief. What seemed to keep her going were her preparations for a climb up Kilimanjaro. I remember punching the air when I received a postcard from her months later. She had done it! She found her closure. "How about you, Sue?" the mountain whispered, but I did not feel the need to conquer mountains back then.

This meeting seems to be going on and on. We are introduced to Godson, who will be our head African guide. He tells us of the professionalism of our guides and once again repeats the right to terminate the climb of anybody who is misbehaving on the mountain.

I feel I have had an overdose of reminders and warnings. We have had the same information sent to us weeks before the climb. Sue has already urged me to read it all and absorb the avalanche of rules and regulations.

Worse is to come when Godson opens the floor for questions. I am amazed and exasperated at some of the requests when Godson goes through the key item list.

"I do not have a sleeping bag", says one fellow.

"Did you order one?" Godson remains calm.

"No, I did not think I would need one."

Another walker is asking whether he can buy gloves and a woolly hat or balaclava in town. Another one wants to walk in his jogging shoes and wonders why he needs a pair of boots. Some people have forgotten to bring their shades or ski goggles. What do these guys think the advice sheets were for? This is cutting into *my* swimming time. There is a pool out there, waiting to be explored, yet people keep asking silly questions.

I am itching to shout out: "No need for anything, lads. Just go up in Y fronts and flip-flops, and maybe take a spare T-shirt!"

It is hard for me to keep my eyes open as I stretch out on the floor. I can feel John twitching next to me.

"Attention now! I am going through the key equipment list", Godson's announcement brings me fully back into the present, although I am pretty sure John and I have everything we need.

A lot of hands shoot up when Godson asks who still needs a sunhat. How can anyone travel to Africa without a sunhat? I quite fancy the khaki hats with their "I climbed Kilimanjaro" slogan that we can buy for 10 US dollars. My cream-coloured hat will probably turn into a non-descript brown on the dusty trails. Maybe I can buy a new hat as my reward after the climb.

There had initially been talks about group T-shirts, but many people were not keen. So our only group souvenir will be the red and white Action Challenge lanyards for our name badges. I hope we will be wearing them throughout our trip. I can never remember names. Even remembering faces is becoming a problem these days. On the flight out, I introduced myself to my neighbour, only to be reminded that we had done a training walk together just a month earlier!

A lot of people have been creative in designing their name tags and included photos and drawings. My only artistic embellishment is the outline of a butterfly. To me, it is the ultimate symbol of transformation and a reminder that it is time to break out of my cocoon.

John mumbles something about the questions going on and on, so I point out that the questions mainly come from the *men* in the group. Like him, they do not seem to have been keen to read the instructions that were sent out in advance of our trip. As usual, John has relied on me to deal with what he considers boring details: organising kits, injections and visas. He only got involved when I suggested hiring winter sleeping bags.

"We already have sleeping bags!" he objected.

"They are for summer, not winter."

"I'll simply take an additional cotton liner and a plastic bag - that will keep me warm. I will be hot anyway, and it cannot get *that* cold."

He cannot be serious! The temperatures at the summit can drop to -20 C. Sometimes I wonder which mountain he climbed in his childhood. The way he is going about things, I will have to climb to the summit without him! In the end, we find a compromise: We hire both a down sleeping-bag and a lighter synthetic winter sleeping-bag. The latter is cheaper, which appeases him somewhat. John says that he cannot remember that such a fuss was made last time - of course he does not remember. I bet his mother did all the running around for him. Just like today, he just had to show up.

I was one of the first to volunteer when our school announced the pioneering adventure of climbing Kili. I was generally a timid goody goody, but figured this was my last chance to do something daring before being sent over "home", as my parents liked to call England.

I still have vivid memories of the trek: the long marches, the patience of our guides as they herded a group of school boys up the mountain, the burning sensation in my feet when we crossed the snowline, and I encountered snow for the first time...

I look around the room. Our fellow-trekkers tend to be in their 20s and 30s. Only our Action Challenge leader Steward and one other trekker are older than John, but age has never bothered him. Inside, John is still the 9 year old boy who first climbed Kili in the

1960s and was apparently told off for racing down the mountain.

Although I am 8 years younger than John, I have never had his energy. I have had to work hard to improve my fitness levels. They say it is no fun climbing a mountain like Kilimanjaro without training, although every year people are foolish enough to try.

"I have no doubt that you will get to the top. You are far too stubborn to give up. But how will we get you down again?" John regularly reminds me of the occasion when I tried to slide down from a large Namibian sand dune on my bum because I was scared of losing my balance. Even I know that this approach is not a feasible option on melting scree - so I have asked my fitness instructors to incorporate a lot of balance training.

I remember bursting out laughing when I was first told to hold a plank position while my feet were resting on a giant gym ball. I was then instructed to roll the ball towards my stomach and back out again - great for core stability apparently. I was also supposed to be able to squat on a *Bosu* ball which wobbled like jelly as soon as I put one foot on it. The instruments of torture have clearly become more refined since I did PE at school! However, I have learned how to strengthen the all-important core, quads and glutes, biceps and triceps, and other unpronounceable muscle groups. After at least 100 gym sessions, I can now apparently do more advanced exercises than the ones required for climbing Kili. If only my PE teachers could see me now!

John has opted for a different training schedule of course. He says cycling and kayaking are the best preparations for the challenges ahead. His specialist training consisted of two walks last month. He also keeps harping on about the hike he did in the Austrian alps last August. He says I should have accompanied him rather than taking a cable car to a glacier, but in contrast to him, I got the first feel of what it is like to walk on frozen snow at altitude. My lungs were fine, but my feet developed a life of their own. Some of our fellow-trekkers have decided to walk without hiking sticks, but there is no way that I am attempting the Kili climb without this extra pair of legs.

    I am really pleased that I have finally found an activity we will hopefully both enjoy. I have long given up cycling with John, as he always leaves me trailing behind. I then have to watch him cycling in circles at the top of a hill, waiting for me to catch up, teasing me about the snails that may soon overtake me. I love walking, whereas John prefers to march. He will only stop when he has reached the highest point. For him, it has only been exercise if he has worked up a good sweat.

    Due to the random effects of altitude sickness, it is often not the fastest or fittest who make the summit of Kilimanjaro. I can think of no other adventure where I have a realistic chance of keeping up with John. Being slow is meant to be an asset rather than a liability. I have recently heard of a group of trekkers where none of the rugby-playing men made it to the top, whereas all the girls got to the summit. The higher fat content in women's bodies apparently makes it easier for us to adjust to the altitude - finally some good use for the fat reserves in my expanding waistline.

    Godson says that he will need to take our oxygen levels and pulse rates. I look for John, but he is gone. Typical! He can never sit still for long. Godson says he needs a baseline for the readings on the mountain to check how well our bodies are adjusting. My oxygen level is 94%. I breathe a sigh of relief. This seems to be about average. Looks like my iron reserves are holding up. I still shudder when I think back to my non-stop periods twelve months ago. The GP said it was a sign that I am approaching the menopause. I am puzzled by my resting pulse of 103 though. I keep looking over Godson's shoulder to see other people's readings. No-one else's pulse rate is in three digit figures. How odd. I do not feel particularly nervous right now. Maybe I have got so used to my pre-climb nerves that I no longer notice when I am tense.

It would help if John would not keep disappearing. He casually saunters back into the room towards the end of the test.

Godson makes no comments about any of the readings. He says we are all individuals, so there may not be a right or wrong here.

I keep reminding myself that I am well-prepared for what lies ahead. I have picked the *Lemosho* route because it is meant to be a scenic non-technical climb and not as touristy as the famous Coca-Cola route. It is also a route with a high summit rate. Apart from scrambling up the Barranco Wall and summit night, there should be nothing to send my adrenals into overdrive.

I know from experience that being mentally prepared is half the battle. I once stopped just below the summit of Lion's Head in South Africa because I had expected a leisurely walk and was faced with climbing ladders up steep rock faces. The image of the summit just above me and yet out of reach haunted me for years. Thanks to John, I got a second chance to conquer that mountain.

This climb has to work the first time though. John says that he is fed up with long haul travelling, so I have promised him that this will be our last Africa adventure.

The Adventure Starts in Earnest

A last breakfast in luxury: omelette with cheese, peppers and mushrooms, cereals, toast and fruit juices - I tuck in heartily. They have a saying in Sue's country that it will rain if people do not finish what is on their plates. If it should rain on our track, it will not be my fault!

The long slog ahead is always on my mind. I can feel a tingling down my spine - a quiver of fear mixed with anticipation.

We have taken over the entrance hall of the hotel once again. A mountain of duffle bags, rucksacks and large plastic sacks announces our imminent departure. I imagine there are a few guests and members of staff who will be breathing a sigh of relief when we are gone.

I hope I have stayed within the weight limit - 14 kg for each duffle bag, one kilo less than the initial instructions said. That seemed plenty, until we got our sleeping bags and Thermarest mattresses.

"I bet I have got the heaviest bag here", my fellow trekker Grant says. I lift up his duffle bag and compare it with mine. This will be a close call. Steward will be the ultimate judge as he weighs our bags on a hand scale. It is a routine affair, until he comes to my bag.

"Oh, this bag is heavy!" In fact, I am 2kg over the weight limit, and so is Grant. We either need to find fellow trekkers who can carry part of our items in their bags or get rid of the excess. I rummage through my duffle bag. There is nothing in here that I want to leave behind. John's bag weighs exactly 14kg, so he cannot help me out. I have no choice but to reduce my load. More and more snacks are disappearing into the big plastic bag that will stay behind in the hotel. By the third weigh in, I am finally in the clear.

There is a sprawling octopus of bags and rucksacks in the main foyer, with ours at the bottom centre. Latecomers are piling more bags on the growing heap. How easy it would be for a bag or two to get "lost". I take a deep breath, suppressing the growing fear that our bags will be stolen in the chaos. Nobody seems to be in charge here, and Steward urges us to get ready and loaded up. With the time past nine, the heat is increasing.

"We should already be on the road by now," I hear irate comments.

The drivers and porters pick up the bags and load them with gusto onto the people carriers that brought us from the airport. "Plan of God" is the name daubed on one of the vehicles.

I watch as the bags are being stacked on the roof. Climbing poles are coming loose and water bottles are clanging about - and we are not even moving yet.

Will we find our bags at the other end? Sue has done all the laborious packing of sweeties, eaties, and more importantly, kit like head lights. She has already disappeared into one of the wagons and I find myself in the other, sitting next to the team medic. He says that he has come to do something different by looking after our group as well as climbing Kili. I can imagine that this is an exciting challenge for any young doctor! I wonder what would happen though if he has a bad fall affecting limbs, or develops altitude sickness. Apparently, Action Challenge have it all covered. They would fly out another doctor. In the meantime, Steward and another Action Challenge member would look after us.

I decide to travel in the bus named "Plan of God". The idea of walking an ancient pilgrim's path like Santiago de Compostela has always appealed to me, but at this stage in my life I cannot take a 6 week break. A 7 day "vertical" pilgrimage is much more feasible - and more exciting. I cannot wait to explore Kilimanjaro for myself. I have read that we will be climbing through all climate zones. Where else on earth can you do that in such a short space of time?

I look for John, but he has joined the second minibus. There is no room left for manoeuvring once we have all squeezed in. We are told to make sure that we are wearing our seatbelts, but many are either non-existent or not working. I am not sure how much good they would do anyway. One sharp brake, and we will be buried under the luggage that is piled up in the back of the bus.

Soon we have left Arusha behind us. The landscape is flat, apart from the mountain on my left that is shrouded in mist. It is impossible to tell whether there is any snow at the top, but the mountain does look impressive and somewhat mystical.

"Is this Kilimanjaro?" I ask my neighbour Lara, who is the trip coordinator.

"No, Kilimanjaro lies on your right."

No matter how much I crane my neck, I cannot get a sense of the shape of Kili. There does not seem to be another mountain. I should not be surprised of course.

When John and I were travelling through the foothills of Kilimanjaro three years ago, I also did not see anything until our guide tapped me on the shoulder and pointed up. I will never forget the awe-inspiring sight: Kilimanjaro's peak seemed to float above the clouds, emitting a warm glow in the evening sun. "Come on up, Sue", the mountain repeated its invitation. An appealing thought. I mentioned to John that I wanted to climb Kilimanjaro one day.

Last year, there was another nudge. "Climb Kilimanjaro for charity", the e-mail said. Maybe this was the answer to my prayer. The doctors had said that the latest treatment I had reluctantly agreed to should sort out my monthly problems once and for all - but at a cost. I therefore needed a fresh vision for my life.

For the coming week at least I will know exactly where I am heading. I also want to prove to myself that my body is still capable of amazing feats.

As Arusha with its vendor shops gives way to arid *bundu*, I watch Maasai herdsmen with their *ghombi* in the distance. They are obscured by the red dust thrown up by the wind playing among the Acacia trees. After a time, I notice that we cross bridges with water flowing underneath, instead of the dry riverbeds we passed earlier. Green foliage and banana palms replace the arid brown plains we have been travelling through.

Our journey seems to go on and on. I have heard that it takes an hour to get to the departure gate for the Lemosho route, but the hour is long gone.

Our bus stops in the middle of the countryside. Are we finally at the departure gate? No, this is just a pee stop. Men to the left, women to the right. We might as well get over any squeamishness now.

We pass tall deciduous trees heavy with foliage, creepers winding around their thick trunks. The air is markedly cooler. A couple of turns and we are here.

At Forest Gate we will have to queue to scribble down our names and next of kin before we can be officially on our way. To our left is a long and loud queue of porters with fascinating and varied wear: old boots unlaced, worn and re-patched rucksacks, donkey jackets, anoraks, brightly coloured cloth caps sitting jauntily on heads - just like Brixton in the 70s.

It is already 11.15am when we arrive. Porters are busy loading and unloading bags, tents, water containers and other kit. It feels as though we have stepped into a bustling marketplace.

My first priority is to find the loos. The last toilets in civilization are squat toilets, but very clean. There is none of the unbearable smell and dirt that so many trekkers have been describing. There is even a toilet attendant who makes sure that the two toilets remain usable.

Every person entering and leaving the Kilimanjaro National Park has to sign a register. I study the long line of porters queuing to sign in. The porters' outfits vary considerably. The lucky ones wear worn-out hiking boots, but it is not uncommon to see porters in old trainers. Many porters are wearing jeans and T-shirts, even though travel guidelines say that jeans and cotton shirts should be avoided, especially higher up the mountain.

I am told that most of the porters in the queue are our porters. We have roughly three porters for every trekker. They all have their specific tasks. There are those who will carry our duffle bags. Others will be responsible for the tents, some will look after sanitation. There are cooks and then there are the porters who are going to fetch the water and make sure it is fit for consumption.

Our group of trekkers is queuing in front of a second window, waiting until our names are called one by one. Once the formalities are over, we are back into the buses for another short ride. Steward tells us that we may take an army truck for part of the journey due to the state of the road.

Instead, we are dropped off on a muddy double-tracked road lined by fir trees. I am disappointed that we are missing out on the army truck adventure, although I later hear that those trucks have no proper seating or suspension.

The porters do not seem to mind the discomfort. I try to count how many of them have travelled in the truck that has stopped ahead of the buses, but I give up. More and more porters are spilling out onto the track, grab a duffle bag and march ahead of us. We are told that they are going to meet us further up the mountain for lunch.

I don my rucksack and adjust the straps to make sure it lies flat on my back. I have learned this on the training walk. I never used to bother with the strap that goes across the breastbone, but what a difference even minor adjustments make. The rucksack now feels like a natural extension of me.

The path ahead is not particularly steep. It is wide enough for a mini bus and looks in pretty good condition. It is dry for the most part, so I cannot figure out why our buses had to stop. I guess the walk will be good for acclimatization, and it is only meant to last for an hour anyway.

I have always imagined rainforests to be humid and dense. I had visions of having to constantly twist my body to avoid getting tangled up in the vegetation. However, the rainforest at the foot of Kilimanjaro resembles a forest in Europe. The temperature is pleasant, as the tall pine trees are shading us from the midday sun. When I look more closely, I notice the squash that has been planted in the clearings.

As we traverse the forested foot hills, we chat our way up into the forest, passing young pumpkins and giant nettles. Trees rustle and crack with life, and I hear squawks and chirps. Straining my head, I can see a family of vervet monkeys. The guides and assistants are very communicative about their lives on Kilimanjaro, especially the responsibility of looking after groups of climbers.

On we go, first up, and then irritatingly down again, cancelling the effort of going up! I am frustrated by the undulations of the trek. I would prefer a straight climb up. I slow down to walk with Sue, trying to distract her from her rumbling stomach and me from my boredom.

The walk seems to be dragging on. It is difficult to guess how far we have walked and how much further we have to go. I am grumpy now, as it is long after midday. Breakfast seems to have happened days ago.

Suddenly there is a roar and cheer in front of us. It sounds like a football crowd when a goal has been scored. John and I turn around the corner, and are faced with long rows of tables and chairs. Most of our fellow trekkers are already tucking into lunch and are informing us that we have just missed the porters' welcome.

John cringes when he hears that they sang the Kilimanjaro Song. We have already heard so many variations of the song on our previous trip. I remember a lanky black kid climbing up a coconut palm tree in Zanzibar, waving his arms about like a well-trained monkey, and singing the song which is called Zanzibar Song over there. Our Kenyan bus driver Peter regularly sang the song, insisting it is called the Kenya Song. It mainly consists of a polite exchange of greetings and pleasantries between a native and a tourist. The song is sickly-sweet and gooey like the Dairy Milk chocolate bars that we are served for lunch. They have turned into hot slush in the heat.

I am still sorry that I have missed the welcome. Tourist entertainment is part of the Kili experience after all. Oh well, there will be other occasions. I am especially looking forward to the tipping ceremony at the end of the trek when the porters are celebrated for helping us to get to the Roof of Africa. I am already admiring their speed, agility and cheerfulness.

While we are eating, we are getting introduced to the seven assistant guides. I notice a mixture of biblical names, English nicknames and unpronounceable African names. I do not even try to remember who is who.

Our very late lunch (it is 3pm by now) is a very English affair with its white sandwiches, green salad, English chocolate and crisps. I long for fresh fruit and more exotic fare and help myself to some cassava. The cassavas taste similar to potatoes, but are more starchy and filling, a satisfactory alternative to the dry sandwiches. However, I am told that the vegetables were meant to be for Ray. The youngest member of our group is allergic to gluten and has to watch his blood sugar levels due to diabetes. Ray is happy to share his food and experiences.

"It will be interesting to see how my insulin pump copes at higher altitude", he tells me matter-of-factly. I admire his determination to live life to the full rather than to be ruled by his body's idiosyncrasies. How often have I denied myself an experience because I was stressed about my periods.

"You should write about this", I tell him. I am thinking about compiling a souvenir brochure with people's memories of our trip. I have already heard so many inspiring snippets from people's lives. I am sure that we will all have great stories to tell. A trek like this is about more than raising money for good causes. It is about personal growth and pushing boundaries.

Some fellow-trekkers say that they have already raised £10,000 for their chosen charities. I now wish John and I had been more on the ball. We have only started collecting donations in recent weeks. My fault really. As usual, John was flexible. He did not really mind which charity we supported, but I was struggling to make a decision. I could think of so many good causes worthy of help. In the end we settled for two small charities, who are supporting vulnerable children in Colombia and Uganda. I love the vision and passion of the founders of In Ministry to Children and Project Shalom. Maybe this trek will inspire me to dedicate myself wholeheartedly to a cause. I am longing to leave a legacy.

After lunch we trudge on refreshed. The ground is damp and the path is now single-file - for walkers only. The climbers now form groups. Our backpacks, red, green and blue, bob like buoys on a windy sea as we follow the path up and down.

I converse with an acting guide called Sam who assures me that I will make it to the top. I enquire as to how he became a guide. He relates that all staff start out as porters, carrying tents and sleeping bags from about 17. After 4 years they can be promoted to meal organisers before progressing to being acting guides. From this point, they go back to further education. They learn the skills to guide climbers and improve their English.

At first I am in the middle of the crowd, but I am beginning to struggle when we have to climb uphill over some larger boulders. The hiking sticks are more a hindrance than a help, and I keep holding my breath as I try to focus on my movements. I do not want to hold anyone up, so keep trying to speed up. I soon lose any sense of rhythm. Then I remember that it is those who take it slowly who make it to the top. I relax and let the others overtake me. Let them rush ahead! They will pay for it later.

The only people further behind are Steward and our GP, Mark, who have stayed with Grant. The poor guy looked decidedly pale earlier, doubling over and vomiting. I pray for his health to be restored speedily so that he can enjoy the trekking experience.

An assistant guide named Goodluck accompanies me. It almost feels as if I have a private tour up Kilimanjaro as I gradually lose sight of those trekking before and behind me. We chat about botany, one of the many topics all the guides need to know about. Goodluck points out the pink impatiens plants which have grown to the size of bushes, but for me the most striking flowers are the red fireball lilies. Their flower heads are the size of tennis balls. Even though they grow in the shade, they seem to emit a warm glow.

I wish I had time to study them more closely and take some macro shots, but I do not want to run out of camera battery before we reach the summit. I have packed a spare battery for both of my compact cameras, but I have read that the batteries can become temperamental at altitude.

I ask Goodluck about the everlasting flowers John was given when he returned from Kilimanjaro as a child. John's bouquet lasted for decades, but then got lost on one of his many moves.

Apparently, the white flowers grow in the next climate zone, and we are going to see them tomorrow. I am definitely going to look out for them to take a photo for John.

No-one is allowed to take plants from Kilimanjaro any longer. In the 1960s, climbing Kili was still an exotic adventure, but nowadays 30,000 trekkers are attempting to reach the summit every year. Everyone I have spoken to back home seems to know someone who has attempted the climb, so I can easily believe those numbers.

When we stop for a short rest, Goodluck points out a group of colobus monkeys, swinging from branch to branch in the trees overhead. It looks as if they are wearing an Elvis costume of black velvet with white tassels. I cannot help but smile.

We talk about tribal life. Goodluck tells me that he is called *Balozi* in Swahili, which means "ambassador". When Goodluck gets excited and animated, I am struggling to understand his accent. As far as I can make out, it is tribal tradition to call the oldest son "Grandfather" and the second oldest "The Young One", even if there are further children. The name choice makes me chuckle. "Grandfather" is probably in his mid- to late 20s, and I imagine his younger sibling as an old man in his 70s still being called "The Young One". Goodluck tells me that the Chaga used to go into the mountains to bring offerings to nature gods, but were the first tribe in Tanzania to convert to Christianity.

Goodluck had to reach the summit to become a guide. He says he has climbed this mountain many times, just like most of our porters. We are clearly in experienced hands.

The biggest group of trekkers on Kilimanjaro are the Germans, so Goodluck asks me to teach him some basic German: *Guten Morgen*, *Guten Tag*, *Guten Abend*, *Gute Nacht*, *Danke*, *Bitte* - i.e. Good morning, good afternoon, good evening, good night, thanks, you are welcome. In return, he tries to teach me Swahili. I love the sound of Swahili. It is so expressive and passionate. I can usually pronounce the words, but find it difficult to remember the phrases, so I keep asking Goodluck to spell them for me. In contrast to French and English, the words are usually spelled the way they are pronounced.

I decide to adopt two phrases for the trek ahead: *Pole pole na makini* (Slowly and carefully) and *Haraka haraka haina baraca*. The latter sounds a bit like "Hurry, hurry, hyena in barrack", but is a Swahili proverb that complements *pole pole na makini*. It means that there is no blessing in hurry. I will have to remember that when others keep overtaking me. All day long, porters have hurried past, even though they are carrying 14kg duffle bags on their heads and a 6kg rucksack with their own provisions on their backs.

"Porter passing on the left... Porter passing on the right." Earlier on, there was always someone in our group who would warn the others to step out of the way. As far as possible, we kept moving to avoid creating a traffic jam. There are fewer porters passing us now, and I notice that the light is fading.

The tropical dusk approaches with a hush in the forest. It will soon be dark. The air is already getting cooler. Sam reassures me that Sue is doing well. I have lost track of her a while ago.

After a few more steep climbs and dips, stepping over thick roots that form stairways, I arrive at *Mti Makubwa* (Big Tree) camp as the light dims.

I am told that we are in tent number 16. To my relief both duffle bags are there. They have been loaded after all! I unfold the air mattresses and sleeping bags to prepare our bedroom. To keep the wife happy, she not only needs food, but also sufficient sleep. She has repeatedly told me that she is OK with roughing it, but I will need some convincing.

"Is the camp far?"

"No, not far now." Goodluck's answer does not really tell me anything of course. I know from past experience that a three hour walk would be considered not far in African terms. Distance is relative when you are used to walking for miles each day just to meet your basic needs for water, firewood and food. I do not really want to hear that dinner is still several hours away. Despite the late lunch, I am more than ready for my next meal. So far, altitude has not curbed my appetite.

Soon it is completely dark. Goodluck pulls out a torch, and I dig out my headlamp. We were not supposed to need an artificial light on the first day of trekking, so I am glad I took no chances and brought mine anyway. I often feel disoriented when walking in the dark. I wish John was here now, but he probably made it to the camp during daylight hours. I reach the camp in time for dinner.

Our tent is near a toilet tent, which means I won't have to stumble around in the dark later. I have been told that "nature calls" increase at altitude.

Sue's headlight gives her an elfish glow. Feeling an old hand at the climbing business, I show her the chemical loo, and yes, the zip has not worked for me either, so I understand her dilemma and stand dutifully outside when she goes in, collecting odd looks from the Maasai watchmen.

I am pleasantly surprised to find a western-style chemical toilet inside a canvas tent. The toilet is the height of a kid's toilet, but that is better than squatting over a hole in the ground. John swears by long drops, but this looks more comfortable. The smell is bearable too, as the canvas lets in air.

I can definitely cope with this. I now chuckle when I remember the crazy dream I had just before we left for Africa. I dreamed that I had locked myself into the only western-style toilet on the whole of Kilimanjaro. Outside, the queue of desperate women got longer and longer. They were trying to break the door down, but to no avail. I was staying put. I saw elephants (!) cycling (!) down Kilimanjaro when I finally came out... Reality is more mundane of course.

The evening meal is very good, considering there is no running water or electricity. We are served meat and potatoes with cooked vegetables and soup - I have lost my usual craving for sugar and am unconcerned that there are no puddings or sweets.

In the dinner tent, one question is asked over and over: "How is Grant?" Over and over Steward gives us the same reply:"He is not well." I know that Steward cannot be more specific due to patient confidentiality, but if there had been good news, Steward would surely have phrased things differently.

Soon our worst fears are confirmed. Grant will have to be evacuated the next morning. Our GP suspects that he either has a stomach bug or an allergy to Malarone anti-malaria tablets.

How devastating to fly all this way to Tanzania only to descend before properly seeing anything. God, this is not fair! The cards seem to have been stacked against Grant from the outset. I knew of course that a 100% summit success rate was extremely unlikely, but I never thought we would lose someone so early in the trip.

We discuss how we can encourage Grant. Someone decides to carry a yellow sunflower, the symbol of his charity, to the summit, to let him know that he is still with us in spirit. I am reluctant to visit Grant to say good-bye, just in case he has a bug.

Who will be next? I wish I had insisted on a Diamox prescription. It eases the adjustment to altitude, but our GP thought that it would mask altitude sickness. This is apparently complete nonsense, but I did not argue the case. One side effect of the tablets is excessive peeing, and I prefer a more natural approach anyway. After some research, I have bought some vitamins that have been especially formulated to help our bodies adjust to altitude. However, John and I seem to be the only ones who are not taking Diamox.

I keep reminding myself that I have not noticed any effects when walking at altitude before. I do not know what people mean when they speak about the air getting thinner. I remember the lid of my water bottle flying off like a champagne cork when I was at altitude 6 months ago - the only evidence that the air was indeed different. Maybe I will be one of the lucky ones who is not affected by altitude.

I have read that some people have the feeling of suffocation when lying down higher up the mountain, and this sounds frightening. Splitting headaches and nausea do not sound like much fun either when you have to keep on moving.

Steward, Godson and Mark walk around to take our pulse and oxygen levels after the evening meal, a procedure that will apparently be repeated after breakfast and evening meals every day of the trip. A nuisance, but also a reminder that I am not young anymore.

Godson asks me how much I have drunk today. I have been very conscious of the importance of staying hydrated and have been drinking at every opportunity. I never thought that I would have to practise drinking enough.

The first time I used my camelback on a training walk back in January, I only managed to drink 200ml during a day's walk. My jaw muscles and throat were aching so much that I was convinced that I had drunk at least a litre. I had to practise at home, and I now know how many sips it takes to empty the camelback. I must have managed to drink the required 3 litres today, but Godson says that I should drink 4 litres from now on. I want to ask him what my readings are, but he has already moved to the next person.

Steward tells us that tomorrow will be a very long day. He has decided to combine the trekking of days 2 and 3 so that there will be less walking required before we are attempting the summit. I would rather trek longer hours while I still have the energy, but I am also apprehensive at the thought of a full-on trekking day.

Back in the tent, I am touched to hear Sue give out little snorts as she sleeps on her back.

How to Eat an Elephant

A porter wakes us at 5.30am to check whether we want tea or coffee. I ask for a flask of hot water, so that I can prepare some herbal tea.

This will make a nice change later on, although the water that the porters are preparing is surprisingly drinkable. The water gets filtered several times and is then treated with chlorine. I expected a horrible aftertaste, but I do not really notice it. Maybe it is just clever psychology, as the water is served in 500ml plastic bottles, which look just like the mineral water bottles we were served in the hotel.

The 6am breakfast offers a wide variety of breakfast options including pancakes, eggs, bread, sausages and a porridge made of maize. If I had known the choices, I would not have brought my homemade muesli and rice milk. I cannot understand why people say that altitude slows digestion. If anything, my metabolism seems to be speeding up. I will need all the fuel I can get today and therefore have a big breakfast.

The daylight comes bright through the trees, cool and dewy. Breakfast is well done - boiled eggs, bowls of porridge, dry toast.

I am having a battle with the air mattresses, deflating and rolling them up into impossibly tight bags that will only accommodate a totally drained mattress. Sue blithely explains that they are self-inflating and -deflating. Larf.

The next battle is eaties - dozens of packets of all kinds of organic nibbles are floating at the bottom of my bag. I have no appetite for them, but hopefully Sue will polish them off. My headlights, my compass and medicines of every description are contending with the nibbles for dominance in my lucky-dip of a bag.

Sympathy for our porters is short-lived as Steward is summoning us. We are off. We have been briefed - time to step into more wet forest.

I am disappointed that there is no time to explore Big Tree camp, as we are leaving at 7am. I had hoped that there would be time to speak to other trekking groups and swap stories. I have not even had an opportunity yet to write in my travel journal or to read a book, but after today the pace will hopefully slow.

Goodluck told me yesterday that we are going to scale a hill called the Elephant's Back, and so the first 6 hours go steadily uphill. Steward says that climbing Kili is like eating an elephant. And how do you eat an elephant? "One bite at a time" of course. So the only way to deal with this steep hill is step by step.

I am soon out of breath and grateful for any excuse to stop - like taking a picture of John's everlasting flowers. They look a bit like edelweiss with their silvery leaves and small white flower heads. Quite plain and unassuming really. I prefer the fireball lilies, but I guess they would not like to be exposed on the increasingly barren hills and probably need more fertile soil than the mountain offers up here.

There are plenty of porters to let pass. The path is too narrow to keep moving when they are trying to overtake. I am getting told off for stopping when the porters are still a few bends behind, but I need these rest stops. One porter makes me smile. He struts past, carrying a big boom box in addition to the kit he has been asked to carry. I can still hear the music blaring long after he has passed. It seems easier to walk in step with the music, but eventually the music fades.

Roots contrive to trip me on unwary steps. Shortly after mid-morning, I become aware of the sky, sun and clouds as the forest drops behind. Now we are among shoulder-high bushes with bright red flowers. The change is startling and sudden. We are ascending the Shira hills according to my little map of Kili - more Tolkien's Middle Earth map than Ordinance Survey.

As I tread on, Steward remarks on the long straggly moss growing on the lee side of trees: "*Old Man's Beard* we call that in the Highlands. It grows in areas far away from roads and pollution." The air here must be very uncontaminated.

Now I am aware of the sun, I douse myself with factor 50, making sure my sunhat covers my neck and my shirt sleeves are rolled down. Sue would be proud of me. She is always lecturing me on the importance of sun protection, even though I keep telling her that my skin can hack it because I was born in the tropics.

I am aware that I have become the weakest link in the group. I can no longer hold a conversation when I am walking. My rucksack seems to be filled with lead, even though I have practised walking around with a fully loaded rucksack and hiking boots whenever I could in recent months. How can I still be so unfit after months of training?

I feel a mixture of relief and embarrassment when Steward decides to take my day pack. He says it is good training for him. Steward is around 15 years older than me, but reminds me a bit of Indiana Jones in his attitude and demeanour. I envy John, who has joined the rear guard and is able to keep up a casual conversation with Steward. The two of them might as well be strolling around Hyde Park.

Bees hum as they buzz around the bright flowers and swifts dart by over bushes, which look like stunted eucalyptus and rhododendrons.

I hang back to encourage Sue, and truth be known, the pace is tough.

I listen to a conversation between Steward and a fellow trekker from West Essex, who discuss football, companies, management and management concerns. New areas for me, but they take my mind off the gruelling pace.

More *pole pole* from Steward with commentaries on other Action Challenge tours like Machu Pichu and the Great Wall of China - both of them apparently easier than Kili. Why did Sue have to pick the hardest trek?

My pace is now wearingly slow and I feel fatigued when we pass through a gap. We are on the far side of the Shira hills and descend onto the plains below with a startling view of the Kili crater white and pristine in the distance.

The tents and huts of Shira 1 are gleaming bright yellow and orange below amongst low-lying bushes - our lunch stop! It is still warm, but I can sense the thin air and so want to take the weight off my legs.

When we finally reach the top of the Elephant's Back, my body jolts awake as if it has been given a caffeine shot. I can carry my own load again as we are walking down towards the Shira plateau. It looks like my body is finally getting used to trekking. I can already see Shira 1 camp. This was originally meant to be our stop for the night, but is now our lunch stop. As usual, distances are deceiving, so it still takes me an hour to get to the camp.

I throw myself on the ground outside the canteen and try to get some sleep. I am vaguely aware that Sue has finally arrived with Steward, but I do not have the energy to be her cheerleader. Guides are trying to encourage me to get up and go into the canteen. I currently prefer sleep to food, but oblige.

Lunch is already being served, but rather than rushing in immediately, I first follow the strict cleansing routine we have adopted to avoid the spread of infections. Before every meal, we need to wash our hands as thoroughly as doctors and nurses, making sure we get into every skin fold between our fingers. This is followed by the liberal application of antibacterial gel.

    A porter passes me a bowl of hot water and soap. As I bend down to wash my hands, the water turns red. Blood gushes out of my nose. I am taken aback. I usually only get nose bleeds when there are extreme temperature changes, but the temperature has been fairly stable today. I feel helpless, as the blood keeps pouring out of my nostrils. I gesture to one of the porters to bring me a cold water bottle to put on my neck. It seems to take forever until the bleeding finally

subsides. My neck is sore. I need to be care
now on and avoid sudden head movements.

    This episode has cut into my already shortene_
lunch break. Lunch consists of a lot of pasta today. I know that my body does not respond well to too much wheat, but I cannot see an alternative form of carbs. It is too late anyway to ask the cooks to bring me something else. I hate having to rush, but I do not want to hold up the group. We have another 4 or 5 hours' walking across the Shira plateau this afternoon. Part of me wishes we could stay here. It would be nice to have time to relax and finally write into my travel journal, read or even start knitting my scarf. At least the landscape looks much flatter, so walking should be easier this afternoon.

Revived, I set off. I am able to maintain a slow rhythm with the help of my sticks. Assistant guide Sam is with me again, but I cannot manage a conversation. He presses on me the need to drink water, although the thought of drinking 3 litres is repulsive.

Steward advises me to simply think about being on a sunny beach somewhere, but one purpose of this trek is to learn to be present in the moment. I do not want to escape into a fantasy world. I had imagined that I would spend my time trekking in prayerful reflection. I even envisaged belting out some of my favourite songs when faced with nature's majesty, but this will have to wait for later. For now I have to concentrate on every step and breath. I notice that even John is quiet now. He suddenly looks his age.

Sue says she needs some plastic bags out of my rucksack to go to the loo. I throw down my rucksack: "You get it!" I am still fuming over all the eaties in my bag. I am too soft on her. She should carry her own stuff. After all, this trek was her idea. Sue looks alarmed and on the verge of tears. I relent and bend down to get the bags for her. My calves are aching.

Lord, what have I done, dragging John out here? He is clearly not enjoying this experience. He is only here because of me!

Yet weak as he is, John is soon out of sight again. It is discouraging to always be trailing behind, but everyone is trying their best to encourage me. My fellow-trekkers are taking turns to accompany me and chivvy me along. I am told over and over again that I need to look after myself; nuts, raisins and energy bars are passed my way. I am also told that I must drink, so I obediently stop to take another sip of water. I feel like a child in the company of concerned mums and dads. I really do not know where all the food and drink goes that I am consuming. I seem to be constantly hungry and thirsty.

I notice that Godson watches me closely. He points to one of my fellow trekkers and asks "Do you know her name?" No, I do not. I have to look at Kili Kate's name badge. Godson is probably checking for signs of altitude sickness. Maybe he wants to know whether I am hallucinating. I want to tell him that I never remember names or numbers, and tend to recall stories and pictures, but I do not have the energy right now. I need to focus on my breath. I just need to get my breathing sorted and stop holding my breath, and I will be fine.

I am aware that my arms and legs are beginning to move out of sync, making me swagger like a drunk. I keep reminding myself that this is just like every day walking with sticks: Left arm and right leg, right arm and left leg. The more I think about my movements, the less coordinated my body becomes. Maybe I should have stuck to the cross-country trainer at the gym rather than doing my cardiovascular training on the rowing machine.

I push on with Sam, still wearied. When Sam asks if I need my rucksack carrying, I let him carry it, so that I can up the pace.

The Shira valley is full of lava rocks and has minimal vegetation, apart from low bushes and shrubs. The valley floor is dotted about with the everlasting flowers - only found here. They are growing on a plant similar to a daisy, but the flower heads are 2-3 times larger and the petals have a mauve hue. I resist the temptation to pick some even though I still miss my bouquet of flowers from my last trip.

Even though my backpack is once again being carried for me, I do not seem to be able to speed up. I have walked much steeper paths before, so how hard can it be to put one foot in front of the other and climb over a few small boulders? There is no way now that I will reach Shira 2 during daylight hours. Will I ever see a camp at daylight, or will I be destined to limp in after dark day after day? At least I can see where I am heading today. The camp is just over the next ridge rather than hidden in the forest like Big Tree camp.

Soon everywhere is shrouded in the dusky haze as the African night approaches. Sam is pushing on with his odd gait - almost a limp. I feel guilty that he has to carry an extra load, so I reclaim my rucksack. Rock ledge after rock ledge later, I see lights and tents. I have arrived at Shira 2! I shuffle to our tent, unroll the sleeping-bags and mattresses and lie down, indifferent to the bustle around me.

Steward tells me that he has asked some porters to come down and help me.

"All I have left to carry are my sticks", I protest, but soon I am glad that Steward has ignored my objections.

It suddenly becomes impossible to move. It feels like my hiking boots are filled with lead, as I try to drag my body another step towards my destination. The porters have come to my right and to my left, so that I can lean on them as I am creeping forward. An acquaintance has commented that Kilimanjaro may offer me the opportunity to experience labour pains, just in a different way than I have always imagined - but I did not expect to go into labour so soon!

The camp does not seem to get any closer. It may be in viewing distance, but might as well lie on the moon. An invisible wall seems to be separating us. I can feel my heart racing. It feels as if I have just sprinted rather than crawled up the hill. I would be grateful for a pulse rate of 103 right now. It feels like mine has doubled in speed. This is what I have always imagined summit day would be like: a fight for every single inch. How will I cope then if I cannot cope now?

"You can do this. You just have got to keep on moving," the voice of encouragement whispers. It is increasingly being drowned out by another voice that tells me to give up: "You cannot do this any longer! What is the point of your self-inflicted suffering?" It is hard to swallow. I do not know how long I can hold back the tears, but I cannot afford to cry. It will only sap my strength. *"Pole pole na makini"*, I remind myself. As long as I keep moving, I am going to get to that ridge. Every step, however small, counts. *Haraka... haraka... haina... baraca... Pole.... pole.... na.... makini.... Haraka..... haraka..... haina..... baraca..... Pole...... pole.......* One final step. I am here!

I am shaking violently now. I am trying to stop the flow of tears, but they insist on having an outlet. Steward offers me a shoulder to sob on, so I can hide the worst of my outburst from the porters. This is so embarrassing.

"Now you need to dress up in all your layers and have some food. I know it is tempting to simply lie down, but you cannot do that just yet", Steward says in his calm, reassuring voice. Lie down? He must be joking! I am starving! Whatever fuel I have put into my body today seems to have been burned up completely.

I am told that John has gone straight to our tent. He is fast asleep when I enter. It is a sure sign that John is not well if he prefers sleep to food. Our GP Mark says that he will take care of John, so I just need to focus on getting myself ready for dinner. I put on my winter gear: two layers of fleece, the down jacket, gloves, hat. I feel much warmer now.

There is a voice penetrating the fog in my brain, but I am not going to respond. I am going to stay here and sleep. I need my sleep. When will the voice finally shut up? "John Irving, you need to go to the dinner tent and not go to sleep." Mark is not taking no for an answer. He should have joined the army! It takes great effort to obey and go.

It is definitely much colder up here at Shira 2 than down at Big Tree. I never noticed the drop in temperature when I was walking. We have walked 15.2 kilometres today, and have gained 725 metres in height. We are at 3,868 metres now - still a long way to go to the summit.

I notice that the stars are out, but all I care about right now is finding the dinner tent. Food, glorious food! I cannot help but sigh throughout dinner, partly from exhaustion and partly from contentment. Some people are beginning to make jokes about having yet another soup, but I am more than happy to have soup and any other food that is on offer. I have earned every bite today.

John decides to go to bed straight after dinner, while I stay for the trekking briefing. Godson and Steward say that tomorrow will be tough. We are going to trek to Lava Tower, where we are all likely to feel the effects of the altitude. Even Godson says he will feel changes in his body. I thought Steward has said that walking will be easier after today? I better make sure that I get some sleep!

Sleep is hard to come by tonight. I keep slipping off the Thermarest mattress and get entangled in my silk liner and sleeping bag. In the end I have to wake up John and ask him to untangle me. John is teasing me and offers his good-natured assistance, which must mean that he is recovering. Thank you, God!

No sooner have I made myself comfortable than I need the toilet. I peel myself out of my sleeping bag and sleeping liner and don my fleece jackets and down jacket. Now where did I put my light? Where is the second shoe? Despite my headlight, I stumble over a tent line when I step out of our tent. What a palaver! I vow to wait until the next morning for my next toilet trip.

At around 3am, the porters are starting to prepare breakfast. Lights are flashing, people are laughing and chatting. How can anyone stay asleep under these conditions? I cannot wait for morning.

Crossroads

I am woken in the morning by the camp bustle. It must be tea time.

The sleeping bag feels cosy and comfortable. I do not want to get up just yet. I do a quick body scan. No stiffness or soreness. The Pilgrim Oil that is supposed to keep muscles supple has done a great job. However, I notice a tightness in my chest and head, probably due to blocked sinuses. This will make it harder to breathe through the nose, but given the ordeal yesterday, I am in OK shape.

I peel myself out of the sleeping bag and silk liner and look for my clothes. I wish I had developed a workable routine by now. It takes effort to deal with the daily packing chores. I reshuffle some of our belongings to make it easier to close my bag. I will probably regret this tonight, but I do not have the energy to wrestle with the wretched zip right now. I need to refuel at breakfast. I can hear John cursing as he tries to deflate a Thermarest mattress outside the tent. It looks like the mattress is going to win the wrestling match. I know that it will only take a tiny spark to ignite an argument between us, so I grab my thermos and head to the dinner tent.

I am wrestling once again with the air mattresses. I finally find a way to deflate the things by sucking the air out of them.

Mindful that I am supposed to drink 4 litres today, I decide to drink the litre of herbal tea that I had prepared yesterday morning. I cannot believe that it is still hot. The thermos will definitely come up with me on summit day! I have read that it is hard to stop water supplies from freezing, so here is a way to ensure that I will stay hydrated.

When I mention my tight chest and head to Steward over breakfast, he asks me to see Mark. I hope this does not mean that I cannot continue with the climb, although a few extra hours in the camp would be nice. Mark listens to my chest. He says there is no fluid on my chest and gives me the all clear. I can fight another day.

I go back to the tent where John is struggling with packing the rest of his belongings. We really need to get more organised tomorrow. We are holding everybody up, and John now has to gulp down his breakfast.

I step out of the tent and look up. Wow, how did I miss this earlier! The summit is just ahead of us. I know that distances are deceiving, but it is great to be reminded what we are aiming for. I had almost forgotten why I am here. I have got to take a photo of this stunning view: a barren landscape strewn with boulders and low shrubs crowned by a white peak. I rummage for my camera, but by the time I have located it, the summit is shrouded in clouds. What a shame. If only I had looked up earlier rather than fretting about blocked sinuses and packing chores. But the mountain cannot play hide and seek forever. I expect that we will see much more of it as our hike progresses. I don my rucksack, sunhat and sunglasses. Once again there is no time to hang around in the camp and chat to other travellers.

"No crying today, OK?" a porter says as I am getting ready to follow Steward and my fellow trekkers.

"I will try my best." This is so embarrassing. I wonder whether he was one of the men who came to my rescue yesterday evening. I am not even sure I said thank you to my helpers. I wish I could remember who is who. I even find it hard to identify Goodluck this morning.

I hope I am not turning into a whining neurotic woman who ruins everyone else's trekking experience. We were told on that training walk back in January that we need to adopt a positive mental attitude to make it to the top. So no tears today, even when the trek gets challenging. Luckily, the path does not look very steep at the moment.

A hearty breakfast and we are off, heading across the sparse Shira plateau covered in lava boulders with everlasting flowers and shrubs still popping out on the lee side. My sticks help me to push on as I keep pace with the main group, exchanging comments with some fellow trekkers.

I am feeling the pace and my muscles are aching. I wonder how Sue is coping? I am angry at my thoughtlessness. Why have I not waited for her?

I am falling behind as soon as we have left the camp.

"You have to keep up today, Sue", Steward says. It is apparently too dangerous for me and the group if I lag behind at this high altitude. The group is already 5 minutes ahead of me. As long as I can keep a steady pace this morning, things will be OK though. I try to stay calm and relaxed and not let Steward's words put me under pressure. He has walked ahead to join the main group and seems to have no trouble catching up. Why can I not follow his example? I want to be part of the group rather than forming the rear guard once again. I am missing out on all the banter and fun. The experience reminds me of school sports. No matter how hard I tried back then, I was rubbish at sports. Too uncoordinated. Too slow. Too timid. Always last. I was only chosen for a team when there was no-one else left to choose.

"We are called Action Challenge for a reason", Lara, our trip coordinator, reminds me. She has drawn the short straw today and has been asked to stay with me. I do not envy her. I know from experience that it is hard to walk deliberately more slowly than your body wants to move. Yet I also feel annoyed. I do not need a reminder that climbing Kilimanjaro is challenging. If I had thought it would be a walk in the park, I would have hardly bothered training so much! I have no idea why my stupid exercise regime is not bearing fruit right now. All I am required to do is walk. No particular coordination or courage required. This should be fun after all the preparation I have done, but this is no fun right now.

I am already thirsty again. Lara says that drinking one litre of liquid in one go at breakfast was a mistake, as water is only absorbed in small quantities. I wonder whether I will get anything right today! Goodluck is carrying my rucksack, which includes my camelback with water. I keep asking him to stop so that I can take a sip. This stop-start means that I am not making much progress. Godson has now joined us and asks me what the problem is. When I tell him about the difficulty of coordinating walking and drinking, he gives me a 500ml water bottle that I can carry in my waistcoat pocket.

"What's all this?" Godson points to my waist belt. He is right. I am carrying superfluous stuff. I will definitely trek more lightly tomorrow. I lighten the load of the belt by getting out a pack of wine gums. However, all the moisture and flavour seems to have been sucked out of them. They taste like cardboard and take ages to chew.

"They are not the right fuel for you. You should eat a few raisins and nuts", Lara says. No, I cannot get anything right today - but I keep trying. I follow all the instructions I have been given over the last few days: I look straight ahead rather than down so that my lungs can take in as much oxygen as possible. I use my hiking poles, even though I am aware that they are not supporting me the way they are designed to. I seem to have forgotten how to put my weight on them.

"Don't think of the summit. Just focus on the next goal", I am told. The next major rest stop cannot be far away now, although the landscape does not reveal any feature that I would describe as a tower. When I ask Goodluck how far it is to Lava Tower, there is a pause.

"Another 5 hours maybe." Another 5 hours! I thought we were meant to get there for lunch! It is already after 10. I wish Goodluck had been more diplomatic and told me that it was not far now. I try to pick up the pace, but I can only crawl along. If there were snails at this altitude, they would be able to overtake me, as I shuffle a few steps and stop, shuffle and stop, shuffle and stop. John will have a good laugh about this. He seems to be doing well this morning. I am pleased he is with the others. He can fill me in on all the jokes I am missing once again.

I can feel hands rubbing my tight shoulder blades, silently encouraging me to keep going. Where is this Lava Tower? I wish there was something to focus on in the landscape. Just boulders and shrubs wherever I look. Steward has told me that it preserves energy to zigzag uphill in small steps rather than taking the direct way in a few big steps; big boulders are best climbed by facing them sideways. All great advice, but not easy to follow when there is no sense of progress.

"Those who hope in the Lord will renew their strength." One of my favourite scriptures floats into my mind. OK, this will be my mantra for today. The Bible goes on to promise that some of the faithful will soar on wings like eagles, but I think I will have to settle for the bit that promises the ability to walk without fainting. "Those who hope in the Lord will renew their strength... walk and not faint... walk... and... not... faint..."

We have stopped by a large rock outcrop and I sit down and rest my thigh muscles, having been reassured that the rear party is on their way up. I notice Mark walking the other way, with a medical bag and no rucksack. I call out in banter: "Mark, you are going the wrong way," but I know instinctively that this is cause for concern. Somebody needs his skills.

I close my eyes to shut out the outside and rest and nap for a few minutes. My name is being called, and I shake myself.

"John, I want to have a word with you!" Steward calls me over. O no, what have I done? I have been suspended on other occasions for seemingly innocuous reasons like face not fitting.

I notice that Steward is sitting on a big rock just to my left. I hope he did not have to wait too long. He draws me aside as soon as I get to him. I will probably get another reminder that I need to keep a steady pace.

"I guess you will have been expecting this. You will have to go down now." Steward does not mince his words. He might as well have punched me. Go down? Now? It's only day 3! And Mark has said I would be OK to trek today!

"But I have not even got to the first main rest stop!" I protest.

"At the speed you are going, you would only reach Lava Tower when the sun goes down." Have I really fallen that far behind? I can see the rest of the group just a bit further ahead.

"I knew 24 hours ago that you would not make the summit, but I had hoped to get you to Barranco", Steward says. Rewind the tape. He surely means: "I *thought* I knew 24 hours ago that you wouldn't make the summit, but now I know you will go all the way!" But no, one look at his face, and I know that he means what he says. There is no resurrection miracle for me.

Steward asks me whether I want to speak to John before I go down. What a silly question! Of course I want to say good-bye to John and to the group. I cannot believe it is over. Why now? Why me? I have been training so hard! Haven't I tried to follow every single instruction? I swallow down the lump in my throat. I am not supposed to cry today!

I remind myself that there is no point in either crying or arguing. We had been told before we ever set a foot on this mountain that a leader's decision is final, and Steward says that Mark and Godson both agree with his decision. It does not matter that I do not have a headache and do not feel nauseous at the moment. I am too slow to keep up, so I have to leave. I have a duty towards the group. It would be selfish of me to continue holding them up and potentially causing someone else to struggle. Steward says that my porter has already brought my duffle bag. I cannot believe that my evacuation was organised while I was still thinking I was heading for Lava Tower!

I slowly walk uphill behind Steward to meet the group. Why did I not see this coming? Did I really think they would put up with my snail pace forever? Steward has warned me after all. How many warnings did I think I would get?

There are loud cheers when I get to the place where the group is having a rest stop. I am not sure why they are cheering. We are not even halfway through the trek.

"I have decided to send Sue back down", Steward says. I rock backwards and forwards on the balls of my feet as he goes on to say that Sue is struggling because she is having difficulties with her breathing. With his deep, sonorous voice, he is well-versed in giving out bad news. He says that Mark has seen her and is of the same opinion and that Sue understands that she won't make it. Steward would make a great politician. He says he realises this is a wrench for us. My gut twists. There she is, white hat broad-brimmed like Paddington Bear, face lovelier than I remembered, tears brimming in her eyes.

"I want to reach 4,000 metres." Suddenly every meter counts.

"You are already at 4,198 metres." Mark shows me his altitude meter. "Hey, that's higher than the Atlas mountains!"

I did not set out to climb the Atlas mountains though. It is the white peak, which has played hide and seek with me since breakfast, that I have wanted to conquer.

"Did you really think you were good enough to come up here?" The mountain is now mocking me from somewhere behind the clouds. I was such a fool, chasing another impossible dream. I had imagined looking over the Serengeti from up high, watching the sun rise above the horizon while the missing puzzle pieces of my life are magically falling into place. I thought that I could handle anything after yesterday's labour.

"A jeep will pick you up from Shira 2." Steward confirms my miscarriage.

"But I feel well enough to walk to the foot of the mountain. I am only struggling to go uphill." On my walk down I want to finally study those fireball lilies at leisure.

"Sorry, Sue, we cannot spare a cook, and where would you sleep?" The tone in Steward's voice tells me that he is not going to change his mind. What about the aim to have us all walk back down even if we cannot make it all the way up? I have heard that Grant walked all the way, even though he was still nauseous. I am not sick. Just slow. I am battling to keep my mouth shut. If I say anything now, I may lose my composure. It is wiser to accept that I will have no say in my evacuation.

"I have enjoyed your company, Sue. I am sorry that it has to end like this." Like any good leader, Steward knows the kind thing to say. We both know that I have been a burden rather than an asset to the team. Even I have found it hard to enjoy my company today. I should leave as quickly as possible - but I seem to have grown roots.

"Do not worry about anything. We will deal with the insurance. Our office in the UK will call you on your mobile every day to make sure that you are OK." I know Lara is trying to reassure me, but the last thing I want is an expensive mobile phone bill. We have already wasted enough money thanks to my foolish notion that someone like me could climb one of the highest mountains in the world. I do not say this of course. Instead, I thank Lara for all her help. Steward is not the only one who knows what he is expected to say.

I reflect on the hours Sue has spent on organising this holiday and the trip to Austria to practice. Should I have been harder on her? Her coordination has been all out of whack in the last few days. I should have definitely been tougher on the amount of sweeties going up!

We hug, and the group want a photo with Sue - they are genuinely sad that Sue will not be accompanying us up. Her popularity is so evident.

Tears come into my eyes. The "essential" person will be leaving me. How will she take it? She appears to make no effort to fight Steward's verdict. I am too fatigued to display any emotions and feel helpless as authority is weighed against me.

Those who are continuing the climb are trying their best to come up with a catalogue of reasons why going down now is the best thing that has ever happened to me.

"You can enjoy a nice hot shower." I am not smelly enough to care for a shower.

"A comfortable bed." I am so tired I could sleep right here on the ground.

"You can get really drunk!" All I want to drink is water.

"I'll try my hardest to think of you all while I am partying!" I manage a lame joke. The thought of me celebrating on my own is as likely as me reaching Uhuru, but we are all laughing now. I can see tears in people's eyes, mirroring my own rising water levels.

It is only at this moment that I realise just what Sue means to me - not all pest! A group photo is taken with both of us at the centre - there really seems to be little wrong with her and I am not exactly feeling like a kryptonite man. As Sue seems to have accepted her fate, there is no point arguing against medical advice and experienced high level leadership. Our two fellow-trekkers from the West Midlands assure Sue that they are going to look after me and make sure I make it.

I have got to focus on practical matters before the water spills over: "I think I may have packed part of John's Malarone supply this morning!" Mark says that he has spare tablets, so John will be fine. He sounds like any good GP who is trying to calm an anxious patient.

Someone asks me whether I have something they can carry to the summit for me. There is nothing to take to the top on my behalf - apart from John. Some of the girls promise they will look after him. I am glad that John will have cheerleaders. He will need them when I am gone. He has got to make it to the top for both of us. Only John can now deliver that sunrise photo from the summit. I hope he is listening now, as I explain the camera I bought for this special occasion. It is a sturdy, very simple compact camera which is capable of dealing with knocks (including being dropped up to 3 metres) and minus temperatures. All John needs to remember are two buttons: on/off and zoom.

There is something else I need to sort. I know! The tips for the porters! I rummage through my pockets to find the cash I have put aside for this purpose and hand it to Steward. I want to make sure that the porters get their full tip. It is not their fault that I am too slow to continue. But what about Goodluck and my porter, who now have to come down with me? They will miss the tipping ceremony. Godson suggests that I give them 20 US dollars to share between them once we are off the mountain.

I can think of no more issues that need sorting, so my departure can no longer be postponed. After a dozen and more good-bye hugs and a last hug and kiss from John, I turn away and follow Goodluck and my porter.

And then we are off again. Survival kicks in. I soon find it tough-going as yet another horizon looms. My energies are drained as we push up. My legs are aching, and there is still no view of our next lunch stop.

Suddenly I can see that a knot of climbers has stopped ahead for a rest and are gesturing ahead at Lava Tower, a giant piece of lava, like a great hill in itself. More importantly, there are tents - canteen tents - at its foot.

I stagger on, using my sticks, cross a stream, and walk up the final few hundred yards - I am desperate for a rest and have no appetite whatsoever for lunch.

I drop my rucksack and lie down. I notice that it is cooler, but I am indifferent to the temperature. However, I am soon moved on by the guides and chivvied into the canteen tent. The others are making space for me in the round tent with a clever wooden cross-shaped table. Two tents suffice for our whole gang!

I sit down for tea then lie down on the side and have a blissful rest. I pass out to somewhere else until my name is called and the smell of food arouses me.

I see that fellow-trekker Greg is holding his head in his hands and instinct tells me that he is suffering, so I recommend that he lies down on the free space that I have created.

Soon Godson announces that we are off again. I feel revived but still uncertain that I can hack more climbing.

I focus on avoiding large boulders as I climb down. *Pole pole na makini*. The same rules still apply. I do not dare to look back.

It takes a while for me to realise that I can take my time now. There is no-one to catch up with. The faster I walk, the quicker I will have to leave Kili. I stop and take a deep breath. How beautiful this plateau is! Stark and foreboding like Dartmoor, but beautiful in its starkness. Why did I pay so little attention when we set out this morning? The temperature has dropped to a comfortable mid-teens, and the sky is postcard blue overhead. Ideal hiking weather.

I brace myself and finally look behind me, hoping to catch one last glimpse of the summit, but there is nothing to see but yet more shrubs and boulders. There is no sign of the other trekkers. Maybe I am looking in the wrong direction? It is easy to lose one's bearing in this landscape. Perhaps I am having a private mountain tour again. In a few hours I will be reunited with the others at Lava Tower. I will get rebuked for my negativity and reminded that I need to maintain a positive mental attitude. Of course I am going to the top with everyone - even if it is on all fours.

When I turn and look in the direction that Goodluck and my porter are heading, I see white clouds rolling in towards Shira 2. No, I will never reach the summit. I have to return to the valley. I take photo after photo from different angles of the sight before me, blinking back tears. I want to remember what Kilimanjaro is like. At the moment, memories of yesterday's walk are already hazy like morning mist. I hope I have taken enough photos to jog my memory later on. I will soon have plenty of time for journalizing.

I try to get back into the flow of conversation I had with Goodluck on the first day of trekking, attempting to recapture what is already being lost. I ask him about his favourite Kilimanjaro route. He tells me how much he loves climbing the Machame route. His description makes me want to turn around and climb back up.

The best is now behind me, so I better stop asking questions. I express my regret that Goodluck has to come down early on this occasion. I hope I sound composed. I am usually rubbish at the British stiff upper lip. Goodluck reminds me that he has already climbed the mountain many times: "I was here for you."

Yes, no doubt about it, Goodluck has been there for me - but to no avail. Goodluck could not bring me good luck in the end. I blink back tears.

Luckily, Goodluck and the porter are beginning to converse in Swahili, so I can stop my attempts at chitchatting. I can still keep this morning's promise. With every step down, my energy increases. If only there was a way of turning around and catching up with the others. There is no way of course. Maybe I will soon be grateful that I am off the mountain. I cannot pretend that I had fun today. I am fed up with tedious plodding.

To my surprise, the way goes down. Cool mist rises from the slopes and I find that I can trek down without hindrance.

A little further, the mist clears enough for me to see the flora and fauna. It is not dissimilar to the West Highlands, grassy, heather growing in tufts amongst the rocks, but there are also strange palms/cacti growing in the valley through which our path runs. They remind me of a plant I have seen in the Namibian desert, although the climate is quite different there.

I talk to one of the girls, who has been struggling for a while. Now that the pain has left my legs and I have recovered the pace, I want to encourage her and help take her mind off the arduous walk we are completing today.

The porters with their packs on their heads and larger rucksacks have passed us by, and within an hour we hear a commotion and see the welcome bright canopies of our tents.

The way down from Lava Tower has been refreshing and my legs are lighter, even though the path has been steep and twisting. I realise that sticks are as useful going down as going up. They have helped my knees traverse the rocky paths and streams down to Barranco camp.

Chairs have been arranged three rows thick and the porters are singing a welcome song, the Kilimanjaro Song and probably a local Chaga song, as I cannot identify any words. Sue would have enjoyed this! I am taken by the porters. After climbing with a heavy load on their head and back, putting up the tents and helping with catering, they are now standing in the cool evening air at Barranco and sing with gusto and rhythm.

To tell the truth, I just want food and my bed, as the Barranco Wall is next on the journey. It sounds ominous.

Shira 2 is now within reach. For a moment, I feel as if I can skip down the mountain, just like John did so many years ago, but suddenly the camp seems to begin to spin. I have to stop and take a few deep breaths. "*Pole pole na makini*", I remind myself when my dizziness subsides.

The sign out book at Shira 2 shows that the person who came down before me was just 21. So this is clearly not an age issue. Goodluck writes that the reason for my evacuation is altitude sickness. I guess this is easier to say than "She was so slow that she was endangering the group."

I am told that I will be evacuated together with another climber. The jeep is already waiting. Even now there is no time to explore a campsite - there is no point now anyway. My fellow evacuee is an American in his mid- to late 60s. He tells me that he had booked a 10 day route on Kili, supposedly a fail-safe way to make it to the summit. However, he kept falling and stumbling and losing his co-ordination.

All too soon we arrive back at the gate where our group first set out. A jeep is waiting for my American companion, but there is no sign of my driver. I hope I do not have to stay here long. Being back where I started just serves as a tangible reminder that I have just miscarried another dream.

I sit on a bench and watch a group of trekkers getting their final instructions. They chat animatedly, looking both excited and apprehensive. Was it only 3 days ago that I too was buzzing with excitement? How many of that group over there will have their hopes crushed? It could be any and none of them. To me they all look well-prepared and fit. There is no way of telling who is going to go all the way, or is there? I think back of the start of the trip, my unusually high resting pulse, the overloaded bag. Would experienced mountaineers like Godson and Steward already have picked me out as the one to keep an eye on? If they were concerned, they did not let on.

When I was younger, I was always told that I am too naive. Is this what has tripped me up once again? No, I was very aware of the risks and have worked hard to minimize them. I was well prepared both physically and mentally, even though I had to keep reassuring friends and family that I knew what I was doing. Many people asked me why I was so driven about this. I have no clue right now. One thing now seems certain. The mountain was not calling me. I called myself.

Maybe this is just a crazy dream, and I am still on the mountain - yet the hot sun on my face and the tears burning in my eyes feel all too real. What am I supposed to do now? Tears are threatening to spill out. I have to do something to stop the ruminating. I will have plenty of time for this when I am on my own. I look for Goodluck and hand him a 20 US dollars bill: "For you and the porter."

Goodluck nods, looks over to the porter, who is currently deep in conversation with another porter, and puts the money in his pocket. I wish I could speak enough Swahili to tell the porter that there is money for him in Goodluck's pocket. I debate whether to say something more to Goodluck, but I do not want to question his integrity. This is really awkward now. I should have waited until both men were together. Everything is taken out of my hands today.

Finally, a jeep pulls up. A young man jumps out and introduces himself as Tom.

"You are German, *ja*?" I am not keen to speak German, but another decision is made for me, as Tom rattles on in German. He takes my pulse and oxygen levels and tells me that he will take me to the hospital to make sure that everything is OK. I feel fine now, just very hot. The sun is burning through the side window of the jeep. It is strange how quickly I had forgotten how hot it gets in the valley. I search for my sun block.

While we are driving back towards Arusha, I remember a blog post I had written just before we set out for Africa. I defined a successful pilgrimage as the willingness to keep on walking even when we find ourselves on a different path to the one we want to be on. All I have to do now is to put my own advice into practice. I guess this new "pilgrimage" will be easier once I have some idea of what the new path may offer. I ask Tom what there is to do in the Arusha area. He shrugs. He says his company does not really specialise in "that sort of thing". However, he can recommend climbing an active volcano: "A really tough climb, but worth it!"

I am not sure that my insurance (or John) would be pleased if I now decided to tackle another mountain! As Tom is unlikely to be of assistance, I will have to wait until we get back to the Arusha Hotel - but here is the next surprise. Tom says that the hotel is fully booked, so I will be staying in the Mount Meru Hotel instead. It is apparently nicer and only costs 10 US dollars more per night. Right now, I am not looking for "nice". Any room will do, as long as it is clean.

The traffic is getting heavier, so we must be approaching Arusha. I hear Tom telling Goodluck that he will drop him and my porter at the next crossing and that they should take a taxi back to the office. So it is time to say good-bye to my last trekking buddies: "*Asante sana. Mungu akubariki.*" ("Thank you. God bless you.") I shake hands with both men. I do not know what else to say. It strikes me that I still do not even know my porter's name. I doubt that I would recognise either men if I saw them in a crowd. It is easier this way.

I wish we could go straight to the hotel now. Chances are that the A & E in Arusha is at least as crowded as an A & E in the UK. To my surprise, Tom pulls up in the empty car park in front of a small single-storey bungalow.

"That's the hospital!?"

"Yes, that's the private clinic we like to use."

There is no-one in the waiting-room, apart from the two receptionists. I am called straight through to see a nurse. She first checks my weight - the same as when I started. It is clearly another myth that everyone who climbs Kilimanjaro will lose weight. "If you hadn't wimped out prematurely, you would have lost weight", a voice whispers. I try to ignore the accuser in my head.

My pulse rate is still 103 and my oxygen levels are in their 90s. It is as if nothing has changed in the intervening days. The nurse checks my blood pressure.

"142 over 89 - that's high." The nurse looks at me. "Dangerous at altitude." I am surprised by the reading. I am sure that my blood pressure was OK a few weeks ago. Surely my GP would have never prescribed the pill otherwise?

The nurse takes me through to see the doctor. Dr Adams also thinks that it was my blood pressure that caused my problems. He says that my blood pressure would have been higher than it is now while I was climbing.

"So I didn't have altitude sickness after all!"

The doctor raises his eyebrows: "Do you have a problem with this diagnosis?"

Yes, I do actually. I was looking out for headaches, nausea, vomiting and loss of appetite, and thought I was safe. I cannot remember reading anything about raised blood pressure as a sign of altitude sickness. I do not like its shape-shifting nature.

Tom insists that we are getting a written report from Dr Adams for insurance purposes. My mind is racing. My elevated blood pressure may explain my nosebleed. If only we had spent the night at Shira 1 as originally planned! Maybe my blood pressure would have stabilised again. But hang on, my pulse rate was already abnormally high before I set a foot on Kili. Maybe this means that I already started with raised blood pressure before we set out? Maybe the cards were stacked against me from the outset. Maybe I never stood a chance - just like Grant!

"Vital signs: BP - 142/89 mmHg; pulse rate 102 b/m; temperature 36.7c. She was evacuated from the mountain because of difficulty in breathing. Chest: On examination - normal breathing sound. Needs to observe the blood pressure", writes Dr Adams. At least he is sticking to the facts rather than speculation. I wonder how many different conditions are simply lumped together under altitude sickness.

The bill is very reasonable by Western standards at 5,000 Tanzanian Shillings or 6 US dollars - a sum of money which is of course out of reach for many Africans who live on less than 1 US dollar a day. The waiting-room is still empty when we leave. Maybe the clinic can just live off tourists like myself, who foolishly attempt to climb Kilimanjaro.

We return to the Arusha Hotel to pick up the items John and I have left behind. After checking my passport, a hotel clerk leads me into a small dark room piled high with plastic sacks. They all look alike, but I know I can ignore the nearly empty bags that have nothing in them apart from spare clothes for the celebration dinner. It is no use just picking up my bag, as I threw our stuff into whichever bag was nearest at the time. It did not seem to matter back then. So many things did not matter only a few days ago. If only I had known what I know now!

We leave the city centre and drive back towards Kilimanjaro. At the outskirts of Arusha, Tom pulls into a drive, and I walk through the entrance of the number 1 luxury hotel in Tanzania, dragging two huge plastic bags, a duffle bag and a rucksack into the lobby. Tom is right. The Arusha Hotel is a bit of a hovel compared with the Mount Meru Hotel, where every surface in the grand entrance hall has been polished to a mirror-shine. You could hold a ball right here. This is a place for business suits and evening gowns.

I try to ignore the mirror that reflects my flushed face, sweaty, crumpled trekking gear and dusty hiking-boots. I do not need a reminder that I do not belong here, as I walk over to the reception desk to register. The staff in their immaculate uniforms are too professional to express their opinion. Tom says that I have to pay for my room upfront, so I hand over my credit card. 780 US dollars for 4 nights bed and breakfast! I could not blame the insurance if they questioned the cost. They would probably expect me to stay somewhere simpler - not that I have much choice really.

Grant has come down from his room to form my welcome committee. He looks very pale and says that he is still feeling sick. He has not left his room since he first arrived. He says the internet connection keeps breaking up and that there are mosquitoes in his room. Luxury can clearly not buy everything.

I eat well and turn in. Only one bag and sleeping kit - I am lonely without Sue and wonder how she is getting along.

Tears are welling up as I remember how I lost my temper with her and slammed my rucksack down when she asked for a plastic bag. I should have stayed with her and chatted with her about the house, our next holiday - anything to take her mind off the climb.

Exhausted and feeling guilty, I fall asleep. An hour later I am awoken by my Irish fellow-trekkers chatting away. I go to the loo and call "Good night, girls." There is no response. I snooze, but am soon woken again by girly talking. It is surprising how girls can natter on in any situation.

"Good night, girls", I repeat a little louder, but still no response. They surely cannot continue with such gusto, not after the day we have had.

I snooze again, only to be woken for the third time. I feel for the top zip on my rucksack, looking for my redoubtable cable ties. They come in handy when you want to teach a lesson to noisy campers performing late night Shenanigans. All I would have to do is tie the cable to the girls' outside tent zip - they would have a "nice" surprise when they need the loo! I learned this trick from a seasoned New Zealand traveller down at Lake Malawi, who locked in some lads in their tent after they would not pipe down. But I am soft and relent. *This time.*

My room is on the top floor and seems free from mosquitoes and any other creepy crawlies - the advantage of being so high up. The room overlooks a landscaped garden with a well-watered English lawn. It could be almost anywhere in the world. I do not even know in which direction I can find Kilimanjaro. To my left somewhere I suppose, but it does not really matter. I am too far away to see anything anyway. I can feel a tear trickling down my cheek.

I switch on my mobile. I had originally planned to send updates from the mountain every day. I never did, thinking I would do it tomorrow. What a foolish assumption. There is one new message on my phone. I hope it is not a belated good luck message.

No, it is just a message from O2. They probably want to welcome me to Tanzania and tell me their tariffs. I wonder how much they are charging for receiving phone calls? But no, O2 say that I owe them £10.50. They ask me to ring 0800 urgently if I do not want to be cut off. 0800 numbers do not work abroad of course. Something must have gone wrong with my new direct debit, so a high phone bill is another thing I have worried about in vain...

I leave a message at the Action Challenge office to let them know that they can only reach me via the hotel landline. I also send two quick text messages to my family and a friend, letting them know that I had to come down the mountain, but am otherwise OK. As soon as I have pressed "send", the dam breaks. I no longer care what I promised the porter this morning and cry myself to sleep.

Walls

I feel recovered in the morning, but nervy as I hear what is immediately ahead - the Barranco Wall, which means scrambling and grappling on all fours. I eat a big breakfast and allow myself the luxury of a coffee as I am tingling with apprehension over this wall. I pray and try to rally my thoughts as I fear being turned back. I must make it to the fifth day at least! A sneaky glance at the others convinces me that I am not the only one who is angst-ridden. A few are more quiet than usual. They keep praising me for how well I have recovered.

Steward informs us that Greg has left. He did not want a farewell so departed with a porter the previous evening. I am sad that someone else had to go down, but have to focus on what lies ahead.

Off I go again, with my sticks tied up in my rucksack. I imagine that sticks will be useless when it comes to overcoming a wall. First we descend for a few hundred metres, and then it begins.

I am in the leading group as advised. Steward wants to make sure I am keeping the pace. I hope I won't slow the others down. Now I have become the weakest link and can imagine what Sue has gone through. Had I been younger, I would have probably felt embarrassed and humiliated, but now I don't care. I just want to survive.

One of the first things I notice when I wake up is the sign over the TV: "Free wi fi available here." No use to me of course. Even if my phone bill had been paid, my mobile can only do the basics. It would be handy now to be able to write e-mails from the privacy of my own room - if the internet is working today.

I switch on my mobile. One text has come through: "*So sorry to hear your news. We have been praying for you daily and will continue to do so, and for John as well. We understand the disappointment you must be feeling.*" So I am not cut off yet from the outside world - just from the Kili crew. The tears are flowing again. Breakfast will have to wait.

Soon I feel myself relax. The scrambling around and over rock faces is a lot more to my liking than the constant pace needed to cover distance yesterday. "You are hacking this well, John", one of my fellow climbers comments, and I am full of pride that there is still life in this old body.

Nobody seems to be suffering or needing support at the moment, and on arrival at the rest areas, I am not languishing and loathing moving off any more.

"How do you picture the year ahead?" I was asked at a recent retreat. My image appeared in a flash: A steep mountain, followed by an equally steep decline which ended somewhere in the fog. I knew that I could not live on a mountain top, but I had hoped that memories of climbing the summit would make valley-walking easier. But my body has failed me once again.

I tip the content of the duffle bag onto the bed. I must have overlooked my shoes yesterday. No, they are definitely not here. They must be with John, somewhere up the mountain. I can imagine him cursing when he finds the shoes and all those sweets he had asked me to leave at home.

I cringe when I notice the bag with my summit day clothes: the expensive thermal underwear I got for Christmas, a blue down jacket and the gloves that promise to keep hands warm even at -25 C. I was so pleased when I found them at half the original price. "Still a lot of money", my father commented. And he is right. I have spent a lot of money. I might as well have thrown the money in the bin. I do not expect temperatures of -25 C back in England any time soon. I pick up the dusty hiking boots that I will have to wear for the rest of the week. I would have never bothered to buy the sturdier pair of boots if I had known how little walking I would do. So much money wasted, and so little to show for it! Even the lanyard which we had been given as a group souvenir has disappeared.

When will those tears stop? I pour cold water on my face and decide that it really does not make much difference that my face is red and puffy. I will stand out anyway, and I am hungry now.

Maybe I can raise more sponsorship for the charities if I dress my story right: "Please sponsor me for spending 4 days in the poshest hotel in the whole of Tanzania in worn-out trekking clothes" or maybe "Please sponsor me for all the tears I have cried." I have cried more in the last 24 hours than in the previous year. I hope John is laughing right now. Please, God, at least one of us has to complete this trek successfully!

I feel almost like a normal tourist at breakfast, as I sit under an umbrella on the terrace, and try out the different dishes on the generous breakfast buffet. This is more like a brunch than breakfast. I especially love the fruit selection. The pineapples and mangoes are so much sweeter than anything we can get in

England. It is a shame that Grant cannot join me. It would be nice to have some company and plot some adventures for the days ahead.

After breakfast, I go to the concierge to find out the sightseeing options. They all seem expensive, although there is a Maasai market that is apparently within walking distance. I take a quick peek at the internet cafe. It lies right next to the corridor where delegates are likely to pass on their way to their conference. It is probably better to postpone e-mails and go to my room. Maybe I will feel less fragile later in the day.

I need to get back to my room anyway. How will the insurance and travel company otherwise get hold of me? It really bothers me that I do not know what the insurance is paying. I have read the insurance document, but the explanations seem rather vague and woolly. One thing is clear: They need to be contacted within 24 hours for me to be able to claim, so I hope that Action Challenge have done their job. I hate relying on other people, especially if those people do not bother to keep me informed. Someone should have called me by now! I pace up and down, trying to work off my nervous energy and tension.

Down below in the valley, a cotton wool mass of clouds is drifting in, curling onto the barren slopes. Breaks in the clouds reveal a green-brown bush on the plains of Moshi thousands of meters below.

On we press, finding footholds amongst grey volcanic rock where aloe plants slyly poke out to the lee of the stones and rocks. Streams gurgle past, giving the scenery a European effect.

On the top of the ridge, we have a brief packed lunch of sandwiches and a chocy biscuit, and we are off again - but no more scrambling as we descend on a brownish-red earth path, standing to one side whenever we hear "Porter, give way. Porter behind you." There is a jovial *"Jambo"* whenever they pass with bags on their heads and rucksacks. Their pace, strength and balance is enviable. With little opportunity for other employment, could I in the prime of youth have done what they do?

Godson gives us a talk about the geography and local geology and how the volcano and the Rift Valley were formed, but I cannot concentrate. The views below are terrific. I can see to the end of the slope we are on. Thousands of feet below, bush and habitation are peeping through the clouds.

I am jubilant that we have done the Barranco Wall, but almost disappointed that there will be no more scrambling. From now on, we will have to rely on our legs, and in my case two sticks. Steward says that most parties enjoy doing the wall and actually feel revived doing it.

The sun is hot and I glance south, down the steep slope to Moshi and the grey-green lowlands beyond. Sue would have enjoyed this view! I wonder how she is coping with the disappointment of not continuing, but I must look forward rather than back.

I should have done more cardio-training. I would have found it much easier to keep up. I could have done regular walks in the South Downs with John. I should

have turned down the pill. I would have run less risk of blood pressure problems. I could have double-checked with the GP whether you can get high blood pressure even from short-term use. I should have insisted on a Diamox prescription instead. It would have given my body some extra help in adjusting to the thinner air. I could have shown my GP some reports to dispel the myth that Diamox can mask altitude sickness.

Should have, would have, could have. Should, would, could. Should, would, could. I try to duck from the bullets as best as I can, but there are too many of them. The bullets are followed by arrow after arrow of "If only's". If only I had been more relaxed about the potential side effects of Diamox. If only I had gone to the Altitude Centre to check my body's response to altitude. If only I had been more realistic about my abilities. If only I had never suggested this climb.

I wish the phone would ring, but the phone stays silent. Dr Adams has said that I can come back for a free blood pressure check today, but I have no idea how to get to the clinic. Tom confiscated all the medical paperwork yesterday and has left me without his contact details. People seem to have forgotten that I exist. I am feeling like a caged animal. I have got to get out of this room!

I remember that the concierge has said that I can walk to the Maasai market. I am a bit cautious about his assurance, as I know that the African sense of distance is different to mine, but I decide to set out anyway. It is apparently impossible to get lost. I simply need to walk along the dusty main road which runs all the way from Mombasa to Kampala, turn left at the next big crossing, and I am in the centre of Arusha. I am aware of how much I am standing out.

No other lone white female around this afternoon. No other woman in hiking boots and hiking trousers.

"Hey, I know you!" An African runs towards me. At first I think he may be my porter or the porter who also had to leave the mountain on day 3 because of altitude sickness - but then I chide myself for my naivety. This is just another way to catch the attention of a *mzungu* on her own. I pretend I have not heard or seen him and walk quickly in the opposite direction. Is it really safe to be out on my own, even before nightfall?

The path flattens out and the crater looms bright with the ice, steep and brooding. Is she plotting some malice against us intruding hikers from afar who dare to disturb her sacred peace and cold?

On the way I talk to Ron, who is the oldest trekker, ten years older than myself. He has been able to raise a lot of funds from his work colleagues and is doing the climb in memory of his wife, who has passed away. He keeps stressing that this will be his first and last long walk. Anyone watching him would assume that he is a regular walker. In contrast to me, he is lean and tall and has a long stride and steady pace. He is a good example of someone who does something useful with his time and money. After all, he could have taken a luxury cruise to the Caribbean with the amount paid for the Kili trek.

We trekkers come from all backgrounds. What we have in common is that we all really want to take on the challenge of doing something way out of the usual, and using our funds to benefit those that can't help themselves. I am proud to be with them!

We pass in front of the crater and take photos before going down to a riverbed, where the water is cool and silvery. I am tempted to stop and have a soak, but Steward is hurrying us on, as only 400 metres up on a high ridge our tea is waiting - and a very important talk on the nature of things. I can feel the rising tension as the final climb approaches.

We shuffle up a well-marked route. I pause to look around and drink in the view - there are short bushes and shrubs with thin and twisted trunks and branches rising up from among the grey lava rocks. A lava block rises 20 meters up on the ridge. Shrubs and little aloes peer out of dried out crevices in the rock. Ominously, the ravens are here too, squawking loudly and flapping their wings as we tramp by.

Soon we are at Karanga camp. Today's walk has been a lot less challenging than the previous days. We are only a few hundred meters higher than at the same time yesterday. If only Sue had made it to Barranco, she would still be with me!

I eat well and even consider what sweeties I will demolish the next day - the dry apricots from Samarkand catch my attention.

Steward comes by and asks me if I mind sharing the tent with Ron. He wants to lessen the load the porters will have to carry and save time in organising the meals and daily departures. I do not mind, as Ron is mature, and I don't want the empty space to haunt me and remind me of Sue. With a bit more faith and vision, I would have been more resilient and better equipped to support her in her worst moment.

I wish I knew the customs of this place. I want to assert my boundaries without appearing rude. Where is this market? All the streets look alike, and this does not seem to be a touristy part of town. I am relieved when I find an English-speaking shop-keeper to get some more directions. After a few more twists and turns, I reach my destination.

"*Karibu*! Welcome!"

"Look here, mam."

"Mama!"

"Sister!"

"Please step inside and have a look at my shop!"

The attention is overwhelming. I feel swamped. What was I thinking, coming here? What I am looking for cannot be bought. All the traders can offer are baskets made out of wire and tiny coloured beads, traditional Maasai paintings of proud warriors and dutiful women preparing meals in giant clay pots, wood carvings of animals and abstract soapstone figurines.

Without stopping, I walk up and down the alleys past shops that are no bigger than kiosks. I glance at things out of the corner of my eye, avoiding the gaze of the eager traders. This is what a prey must feel like that is being chased by a pride of lions. Friendly, smiling, welcoming lions, but after my "blood" nonetheless. I should have known better than to walk into a tourist trap. Did I really think I could pretend to be a happy tourist on a bargain hunting mission? I need to get back to the hotel. I need my space. I do not have the energy to wear the mask that is expected in this place.

"No, thank you. *Asante sana*. I am only looking. Not today." Can they not see that I am not an ordinary tourist? I need answers, not trinkets. I keep walking -

step by step. *Pole pole na makini.* I never thought that the survival skills I learned on Kilimanjaro would still come in handy in the valley.

Our tea is earlier than usual. Steward wants us to walk uphill from the camp without our rucksacks to acclimatise ourselves. The air is thinner, and this is the highest point we've been all day. After 20 minutes, we all sit down on a group of rocks while Steward and "Goody" lay down the marching order for the next day.

There is more talk about drinking 4 litres of water a day and not to stop drinking even when the temperature drops, reminders to eat, especially at breakfast, even though at altitude appetite declines for many people. Goody warns us again about unofficial stops, no holding up others behind. He says to look out for one another and to make sure we know our particular group so no-one goes missing or faints while having a pee behind a rock. No going for walkabouts out of camp. Report any signs of fainting, strokes, breathing problems, lightheadedness or pain in feet or legs. Mark will be available 24 hours, as is Lara.

Only one more camp after this. As we are walking back down to the camp, I see Carol stop and vomit. Poor girl! I root for her to make it on crater day.

I feel surprisingly refreshed and confident now that Steward has informed us that the next leg to Barafu is less demanding than today's hike from Barranco, which in itself was a breeze compared to the hard slog and struggle over the Shira hills to Shira 2.

I am admiring the steep view way below. Bright pin-pricks of light indicate habitation, but Moshi town itself is hidden by the dark ridges that frame my view. I have a sense of being cut off from the world below and to add to the eerie atmosphere, the white topped crater floats in the dark sky behind me. A chill runs through my stomach. I am sure that Sue would have made it today and would have been in awe of the sight.

Tom finally turns up towards evening. It does not sound as if John knows what has been happening since I was evacuated.

"I can call Godson on the satellite phone if you want." Tom shrugs, as if to say "No big deal." I long to hear John's voice. I want to hear that he is doing OK.

It takes two attempts to get a stable connection, and John sounds excited. He says he too was not well yesterday, but has now caught "second wind." He says that he is on a spiritual journey and that prayer is working.

"That's great to hear, honey." I wish I could share his optimism. I too wanted a spiritual adventure, but if this is it, I'd rather go without one. I take a deep breath and tell John about all the exciting trips I may do over the next few days.

"I am thinking of visiting a coffee plantation and maybe Lake Manyara. There are quite a lot of options here. I hope you do not mind if I make the most of my time off, even though trips are expensive."

"Of course I do not mind. Enjoy yourself!" The line is cut off, and I picture John striding back across a barren landscape to join his fellow trekkers. I bet the stars are out again in force tonight. I am glad I kept things light-hearted and positive and did not tell him how overwhelmed and lonely I felt at the *Maasai* market today. I am struggling to book day trips. I want to keep extra expenses to a minimum and am definitely not prepared to pay 400 US dollars to see flamingos on Lake Manyara. If there were other tourists, it would halve the cost. There do not seem to be any tourists at the Mount Meru at present, just business travellers and conference delegates.

There is also a trip on offer to Arusha Snake Park. I remember it well from our previous overlanding trip. It was the last stopover before we were flying home: At first I walked away from the challenge of holding a grass snake, but then I changed my mind. I did not want a trip that had started with me walking with young lions to end on a low note. So I went back to the snake enclosure just before closure time, dragging John along so that he could take a picture of my feat. He had of course managed the challenge the first time around - not that he saw it as a challenge. He said that he found the snake "rather sweet." The handler showed me how to hold the snake just behind its neck so that I could control its movements. The snake did not feel cold and slimy as I had imagined, but warm and surprisingly muscular.

"OK, now put it around your neck like a necklace. Do not worry, it won't bite. Just hold it as before." The handler decided to push me even further outside my comfort zone. A group of school children were watching us. They pulled faces and moved away when the handler approached with the green snake, so I needed to be the adult, showing them that there was nothing to fear. John took photo after photo, as my face expressed varying degrees of discomfort and disgust. I never managed to relax, but at least I did what I set out to do. Back then I was growing and going places...

Now I am stuck. Everything I have done today has only served as a temporary distraction, yet sitting around in a posh hotel-room which could be almost anywhere in the world seems a waste too. I wish I had the confidence to believe that if I stick to this path that seems to be leading to nowhere, I will eventually reach a peak.

I wish I was feeling sick. Even a little bit of dizziness would do. Was I really more sick than anyone else in our group or was I making a big fuss about nothing because I did not have the perseverance and mental discipline to see the challenge through? I remember making fun of the American sounding strategy to employ PMA (a positive mental attitude) at all times, joking that I only know about PMT (pre-menstrual tension). I feel that I have been skiving today, whereas Grant is still vomiting and has hardly left his room. Not even a sore muscle as evidence that I was trekking yesterday. What am I doing here?

All I will see on summit day is the silhouette of Mount Meru, which lies opposite the hotel. It looks close enough to touch, but is too far to get to. Out of reach, like many things I have once hoped for....

I thought I would be able to face future challenges with more grace and poise because of what I have achieved on Kili. Why this, God? Why me? But then again, why not me?

I look at Oprah's quote - one of the many quotes that were meant to nourish my spirit while I was climbing. She says that when you come down from the mountain you can either reminisce about the beauty you have experienced or develop a fresh vision and tackle the next mountain. Those Americans are always so optimistic about what they can achieve in life. I am weary of mountains right now. Maybe I simply need to learn to be content with walking in the valley. I cannot see myself daring to put myself out there again, risking more disappointment and avoidable pain. I did not have to climb Kilimanjaro, after all. I chose to.

At least we have raised some money for people who cannot choose their mountains. The financial costs are bearable, but I am not so sure about the emotional costs.

Suddenly I remember the text I have received this morning. I do not have to cope on my own. Many friends are praying for me right now. The problem is that most will still be praying for me up the mountain. I will need to tell them about my aborted "pilgrimage". Here is finally something practical I can do tomorrow!

After dinner I am not relaxed enough to sleep, so I walk out into the cool night and look down into the inky blackness perforated by specks of light below. At the foot of the mountain, I believe I can even see traffic moving, thousands of feet below.

Above is an ominous floating layer of white, all I can see of the crater. It has developed a personality of its own, silent with menace.

I hope that I will be able to make it - no, I must. Too much has gone into this trek: Sue's meticulous planning, the expenses and my ego. I simply could not return to work without having made it. Work has been my biggest sponsor.

Please, God, please! I wring my hands as I know the effort needed in 24 hours' time will test my endurance all the way up.

Sometime later I return to the tent, ready to sleep. Tonight everyone is quiet.

Preparing for Summit Night

I wonder whether the tears will ever stop. I am used to helping others to process their thoughts and feelings, but I do not seem to be able to do the same for myself.

I dread the thought of sitting in the internet cafe downstairs and bursting into tears in front of strangers. I know friends and family will be supportive, but I am not sure I can cope with expressions of sympathy right now. I prefer to share my struggles when they are already in the past. However, telling people what has happened can only be postponed, but not avoided, as I have told a lot of people about our adventure.

I also remind myself that many people never make the summit, even though accounts of Kilimanjaro may give the impression that "victory against the odds" stories are the norm. We unsuccessful trekkers are usually mere cameos in a successful climber's account. We show the hero or heroine's feat in an even better light. Once our job is done, we disappear without a trace...

We are roused early to a brilliant morning with bright views of the foothills far below and of the crater, now looming closer above us. Swathes of mist cruise by, white and damp, then move on, letting us feel the warmth of the equatorial sun.

Visibility is good and the air thin as we trudge off confident that the next camp is only four hours away with two valleys to cross.

The path is obvious: red earth winding through scrubs and boulders of grey. The shrill call of birds is amplified by the stillness all about.

From the crater gurgles a shallow but clear river. Higher up by the riverbank the rocks are stark black, but where the water is flowing they are lighter grey with shining flecks of silver. I speculate what mineral wealth might lie hidden within the mountain.

After a steep climb, we arrive at Barafu, our home for the next 33 hours and last stop before the crater.

I dump my kit and head for lunch. For the rest of the afternoon, I wash, snooze and relax until tea.

I am glad that the internet cafe charges by the half hour. It helps me to be focused and to keep my emotions in check. I type a quick e-mail and press "send" before I can change my mind. What a relief to finally cross off the only item on today's "to do" list - but what am I going to do with the rest of this day?

At Barafu, the adrenalin is kicking in as I look up at the crater, now very near and almost watching us. I am grateful that I have made it this far. I am gearing up to the idea that I am going to do this come what may.

We meet in the dinner tent as usual, but there is now an air of expectancy when Godson announces that the time is coming.

The girls twitter and wise-crack: "The time for what?"

Steward reads out the order of march for the climb. I am saddened that I am in the slow group, but it's what I have expected; I cannot keep up with the fast group.

Steward and Goody remind us to take spare water bottles in case our camelback supplies freeze. I am sceptical. There has been no hint of frost or ice so far, except high above on the summit. But I do as I am instructed.

I fill up the camelback and put insulation against the cold on the exposed tube, which runs from the bladder in my rucksack to my mouth. I fill it with 2 litres - quite enough, as I still have 1 litre remaining from Karanga. I take out a fleece, inner jacket and outer jacket, inner gloves and outer gloves, long johns. I pack them in an airtight bag. I am relieved when a young couple donates AA batteries, as my headlight is fading already. It would not hold out during the night going up to the crater. A few old items of clothing go into the large bag, as they won't be coming up. There will be no more porters. We will be on our own from now.

I spend the day reading, writing, dozing and sleeping, first by the outdoor pool and then on the bed. This is interspersed with a brief dip in the infinity pool, a trip to the generous breakfast buffet and another chat with Grant, but the role of a lady of leisure is alien to me. I need a project - even if the project simply consists in trying to negotiate a better rate for a day trip to Lake Manyara.

No matter what I do, I cannot forget that today was meant to be one of the most challenging and exciting days of my life. For months I have been trying to anticipate the nerves, tension and anxiety just before summit night. I was both dreading it and looking forward to it. This was supposed to be the highlight of this Africa trip. What do I have to share about now? Nothing. Tales of luxury meals, infinity pools and floods of tears make boring, pitiful stories. I feel ungrateful thinking like this, yet no matter how luxurious life is in the valley, it seems bleak. I have been handed a gift box wrapped in expensive and pretty wrapping paper, but the box inside is empty.

It is strange how I never lost my appetite at altitude, but down here I have to force myself to eat. I still have a container full of homemade flapjacks. The flapjacks are about as tasty as cold hardened porridge. When I have finished these, I never want to bake another flapjack!

I will also cancel my gym membership, as exercise is clearly a waste of time for someone like me.

Just as I am about to bite into the flapjack, I spot the first signs of mould. O great, another example of wasted resources! Once again I am wrestling with guilt over all the money I have spent to indulge in a fleeting experience that never came to pass - yet there is also a sense of relief. I can now move on to eating something else for dinner. I decide to eat in the restaurant tonight, but there are still several hours to kill beforehand.

Reading is usually a great way to pass time, but nothing inspires me right now. I notice that the unfinished Kilimanjaro memoire on my Kindle has somehow ended up in the Kindle archives. How appropriate. I do not want to know how someone else conquered the mountain that has defeated me - although I now appreciate the hardships and challenges involved. I would be more interested to read about people who do not make it. How do they cope with the disappointment? Do they cry as much as I have cried in the last few days?

After a late brunch, I lie down. Sleep proves elusive, as on many other occasions when I could have done with a few hours' kip: before the first night shift, or sleeping overnight at airports awaiting an early morning plane, for example. My brain insists on chatting. My thoughts go back to Sue. What is she doing and thinking right now?

The creeping icy fingers of fear squeeze my stomach as concern over making it to the top begins to take over my mind.

The external noises do not help to quieten me. The girls are chatting again! The porters, within their groups, start making a noise too. It starts as the occasional comment, just a word or two, but as the heat builds up, so do the volume and intensity of the conversation.

I can picture them sitting outside, long gangling limbs draped over benches and rocks almost 5,000 metres high, but still Africa - the same greetings, gossip and accusations as at any road or railway junction from Cape to Khartoum or Kinshasa. There are no stalls selling bananas, yams or beans here, but the noise is still like a full orchestra. The temperature must have reached 28 C or more.

Ronald, who has been sleeping with deep breaths and occasional snores, awakes, blinking.

"Noisy so-and-so's, aren't they? Will they ever shut up?"

"No chance", I reply. "Not for another 4 hours, when it cools."

In the hotel lobby, I bump into the elderly American who had shared the jeep journey to the gate. We go for a smoothie in one of the many hotel restaurants.

He says that he is flying back today, as he still cannot sign his signature properly. I am wondering whether he has had a stroke. When I ask him how he has been coping, he admits that he has had the "odd tear" in his eyes. He says he would have found it hard to meet his fellow trekkers again, as he got close to them in the days they have shared together on the mountain. I can relate to his apprehension. Grant and I have been offered a lift to the arrival gate on Friday, but I am not sure that I will make a good welcome committee right now. Going to a coffee plantation is a more appealing option, even though I have never liked the taste of coffee.

After a while I doze off for an extended siesta. I am succumbing to the glorious depths and heights of slumber when I feel a nip on one of my toes. Is this part of a dream? No, another nip, hard. This is for real. Someone is playing a game. I pull my foot slowly in and turn over, catching a glimpse of a ball of fur and long bare tail leaping over Ronald and scurrying up to the top end of the tent.

I curse as I realise that the mountain tent has no opening at the top end and think of all the sweeties that the rodent will enjoy in my bag.

"Ronald, we have a visitor."

"Who?" Ronald raises his head.

"A four-legged friend who is by your head."

Ronald takes one glance at our uninvited guest and dashes out, leaving the tent to the pest and myself. The mouse has an interesting red fur with white stripes on the back. He sits still by my pillow after leaping about, and I have time to retrieve Sue's camera from the bag and shoot some photos.

I swear in frustration as the 'wee beastie' jumps every time I click - of course, Sue's camera is a digital camera, which only takes a picture 2-3 seconds after I have pressed the button - unlike the old analogue cameras, which were truly instant.

I manage three shots before shooing the rodent out into the barren exterior. I hope my inhospitality does not expose him to the avaricious ravens lurking about during the day.

Ronald returns to the tent to slumber. I know I can't sleep, but lie down on the sleeping bag and pretend to sleep anyway. My brain is not fooled, however, and stupid, irrelevant thoughts assail me: about work, Britain, the EU, the coming trip to the coast. What will Nairobi, the city of my birth, look like on my return 45 years later?

My thoughts return to Sue. How is my darling wife in Arusha? I can only imagine the disappointment she must be feeling, as Kilimanjaro is definitely her baby. All the hours she put in to prepare for this, training in the gym, ordering the kit, finding the right travel company, dealing with concerned family and friends.

I am grateful that our brother-in-law insisted that we get some decent kit in a specialist mountaineering shop at Christmas. The new boots and jacket have already stood me in good stead, but what about Sue? She will have to take up another climbing challenge soon to make use of her kit!

Steward has been an expert in reassurance and has said that all is well with Sue. The insurance has apparently already paid for Sue's stay at the hotel. I hope this will help her to relax and have some fun.

Two more days and I will be back down, and we can swap stories. I must do this for both of us and for my sponsorship. I want to hold my head up high at work. My work mates have been the biggest group sponsoring me. I owe it to them. I have to do this, even though the muscles in the back of my legs have already given me a lot of trouble up Lava Tower. I wish I could sleep! I get into my sleeping bag as the temperature drops and light fades.

Ronald awakes in response to both. I mention how envious I am that he must have had three hours' sleep already. He says he has only had an hour or so, as he was lying comatose without sleeping.

I snooze a while, then there is the call for dinner and the tension is building - not just in myself, but in the others too!

Again Steward reads out the order of march; there is more advice and reminders of what we will need. Godson's "The time has come" is greeted with laughter and joviality. This is the last time our pulse is taken.

As I eat, my nerves are pumping. How will I feel the next evening, made it or not, what are the consequences?

For the last time I look down the slope to the lights way below, far from my concerns. I wonder how many others have done the same in an attempt to stave off their anxiety?

I rest for another couple of hours before we are being summoned for the Big Off. It is a last chance to check our kit before the climb.

I am so glad that I have been given spare batteries for my head torch. I debate with myself whether to wear my long johns. They will cause friction and require extra energy, but my legs would be warmer. Same with the thermal undershirt. I am aware of how I heat up quickly, sweat and cool down - I don't want that. However, if I take too little, it would be shameful to have lugged all this kit this distance, leaving clothes and then having to come off the crater due to hypothermia. I decide to wear the long johns, but not the thermal vest.

It occurs to me that if we had left this morning, we could have been back by now and celebrating! But as always, we are doing this to avoid altitude sickness.

Ronald and I amble to the dining tent for biscuits and hot drinks. We are talking, but I don't take in what we are speaking about. With reminders of the time, we take biscuits, make sandwiches and have cups of tea and coffee. There are yet more reminders that last night it was -15 C, so we have to take our ski goggles, hats, head warmers, scarves and of course water.

Up in the first group I trudge out. I am positioned behind Moses, an assistant guide. He is round-faced and big bodied, but his walk is agile. The girls are chatting behind me. Where do they get the energy? I am too apprehensive to talk.

The scenario in front of me reminds me of the Billy Elliot play: We look like miners, as our head lights are pricking the night as we ascend. We trudge out of the camp and along a path that is steadily going up. Steward is wishing us all the best and after more reminders about pace, water, warmth, says he will see us at the top. Stella Point - will I make it?!
In a mad moment, I call out: "It's like Thomas, the Tank Engine. *Shooo Shooo Shooo Shooooooooooooh.*" Steward looks rather concerned and worried. Nobody else responds.

On we go, with lava at either side, a few twists and turns - and we have arrived at the foot of the crater. I look back and down. The last group is leaving camp now and are half a mile behind. They look like a long insect with many eyes worming along the route.

To my right I can see Mount Muensi and to my left Mount Meru. The rival peaks are only silhouettes but are still higher than us.

The path gets steeper and we are now winding up in zigzags. I am consciously economising on my step, slow and short, trying to keep a constant pace behind Moses. I remind myself that I am finally off to the promised land, but it is increasingly an effort to lift my feet to avoid rocks or crags on the path. The path consists of sand - the worst substance to walk on after mud.

In the evening I finally get two pieces of good news: The insurance is paying my hotel bill, and a trip to Lake Manyara now costs a more reasonable 145 US dollars, as two more people have been found for the trip.

I have another chat with Grant. What a blessing to have him to talk to. He always seems to look on the bright side. He says there is a spectacular display of lightning over Mount Meru tonight. I have not noticed anything, as my hotel room faces in the opposite direction. I dash outside the hotel - I still cannot hear a single thunder clap.

I am trying to capture the silent spectacle on my camera, but I soon give up. Without a tripod there is too much camera shake. I neither have the patience nor battery power to experiment. I hope the guys are staying dry on Kili. In a few hours they are starting their final ascent. I feel as far removed from their experience as the thunder is currently from the lightning.

Dealing with What Is

I lose balance a few times, ominously aware that this is a sign of fatigue, but plod on behind Moses. Each time I fall back, I am given a hearty shove that sets me right, but I simply do not have the energy to look around and thank the person who has given me the needed boost.

We stop and rest on a fair-sized ledge and I take a sip from the camelback. While we rest, we can hear the radio communication between our guides and Steward and Mark. I am in survival mode and not concerned too much with what this is about, when I hear the encouraging announcement that we have passed the 5,000 metres mark - we are more than a quarter of the way up!

I reason that if I have "hacked it" this far I can push on to the halfway point. Then there will be no way that I would turn back - even if my legs go dead, I will scramble up on my hands and knees. I have to do it. It is mad, mad, mad, but there is no going back before at least Stella Point. Not now.

I have been observing the peaks of Muensi and Meru. We finally have the same height - almost. I did not expect them to be so high. Meru, away to the west, is having lightning flashes on its summit. It is unreal, simmering and flickering, with streaks of lightning eddying around the top. I have become part of Tolkien's world, and I am Bilbo, helpless and gasping on a mountain slope; in the distance a dragon is emerging from its lair.

Unforgivably, my camera keeps showing "low on battery". I point this phenomenon out to the others in the hope that they will take photos, but I am received with little enthusiasm.

1 a.m. The storm outside has passed. The one inside is still raging unabated.

The others are ascending now. I wonder whether their night is clear. Once upon a time I was looking forward to walking up Kili at almost full moon. I cannot see the moon out of the hotel window right now, but maybe I am looking in the wrong direction. There is no-one here to ask.

I am aware that it is warm and comfortable in my room. I am sure that it will not be as cosy on Kili. For months I have been concerned about what -10, -15 or even -20 C would feel like at altitude. Now I will never know. The thought gets the tears flowing again.

I need some distraction. There is a novel on my Kindle that I have not read yet. Other people have said that *The Bastard Tree* is thought-provoking and inspiring. I appreciate how the book explores the difference between spirituality and religiosity, all too aware how often I fall into a performance trap. However, I cannot relate to the kind of God described in the book, a God who seems to pull out all the stops to help the protagonist to understand what is truly going on. I wish I could relate, but my God is distant and silent and does not seem inclined to tell me where my story is heading.

I wish I could be more excited about the day ahead. I always enjoy getting immersed in creation. I am sure there will be some awe-inspiring views when hundreds of flamingos turn the sky pink. It is just that I was looking for a more active involvement on this trip. Now I will be stuck in the observer role once again.

Some of my spiritually-minded friends will probably tell me that my failure is a blessing in disguise. They have often said that I have never truly surrendered and live my life on my own strength - but did I have to come down from the mountain prematurely to realise that my strategy is ultimately futile? I was very aware of my frailty and need for others while I was still climbing...

We press on. I stick behind Moses. It is grim, but every step gained is a step less to Stella, so I stumble on.

Another group overtakes us and we barge and collide as they pass. I am trying to discern whether this is our fast group coming to overtake or another party. I don't recognize them, so it is an alien group who has climbed up a different route.

We tack up, from left to right and to left, zigzagging. I stumble and am given a good shove from behind - I am aware that without these shoves, I would not make it. If I fall now, I will not be able to get up again.

Sand, rock and loose stones and boulders lie by our way. *Clump, clump, clump.* I am getting weaker. When I draw on the mouthpiece of the hose which runs water from my camelback, no water is coming, no matter how hard I try. I notice that my hands are feeling cold, but it is too much effort, physically and mentally, to get out my under gloves, put them on my hands and get the over gloves back on.

Assistant guide Moses is very obliging, providing a bottle of water. I cannot believe that his hands are still ungloved!

I grab the bottle of "Kilimanjaro wine", as Sam calls it. I force myself to drink, even though my stomach is rebelling at the influx of cold liquid.

Mount Meru's lightning fingers illuminate the summit, and now much of the mountain and backdrop are lit up with an eerie phosphorescent glow. Nobody else seems impressed, and I clump on, dragon or no!

I take another sip from Moses' bottle of water. It runs down my throat, causing me to shudder. It is so cold, that it seems to burn my gut. I dread these water stops. I eat some more nuts, prunes and figs from the Samarkand packet.

We wind up, zigzagging to the left and right, every change of course causing a struggle. I stretch my leg, turning to avoid the rocks. I wonder how long I can keep doing this as the muscle pain bites into the back of my legs...

SHOOOOOH - Thomas, the Tank Engine is coming up the mountain. *SHOOOOOOH, SHOOOOOOH*, there is a lack of coal, pistons are leaking and lacking grease, air steaming out of cracks in the boiler. Yep, that's me. Yes, I am a bit delusional but who cares? If I let my mind wander, it takes attention away from the upward grind.

Can I do it? Yes, I must. I cannot stop now. Meru is still flashing, but less now. Daylight should be coming soon. All will be well then. Dawn - when that great pink glow comes my hopes will rise with the coming of the day. Why are we still chugging along in the dark, sticks tapping and scraping along the ground, our head lights like fingers in the night?

The cold and dark are miserable. I can no longer feel my stomach - there is nothing there, *nothing*. This is not hunger. This is exhaustion!

The backs of my legs groan. Steward is about; radios are crackling and I hear a very welcome "Let's take a break by the next ledge." We stop, and I know it is time for my next beastly slug of water. It flows through my gut like a frozen bullet of mercury.

We are now more than half way up. We have only 500 metres to go!

Welcome news! I won't stop now. I will do it, come what may. I look across at Meru. The flashing has stopped, and it is now virtually invisible behind light clouds. I think I can make out the Meru summit. It is just below us.

Steward continues reading out figures, something about being higher than any European mountain and at the same height as Everest base camp. I can't absorb the stats - I need every bit of energy. I will do it - too late to turn back or stop now.

Although my legs groan I scramble off, once again behind Moses. For the first time I notice that one of the girls is also struggling. I am not able to push up for much longer. Will have to reach the summit soon or pass out. Someone from our group just had to go back down, though I don't know who!

I shuffle on. The crater is black and outcrops of rock go by teasingly slowly. My head spins. How does this compare with walking on the moon? The cold bites and my hands are frozen to my sticks. I wiggle my fingers. They are cold, but I cannot be bothered to stop and get my under gloves out even though I know they would make a difference.

Way below, I see the Moshi lights twinkling and spare a thought for Sue. How will she be when we meet up? Tears all round probably. Right now I am too exhausted to laugh or cry.

We stop on another ledge, and it is announced that this is the last stop before the top of the crater - Stella Point is 400 metres ahead.

On we shuffle, like the prisoners in *Les Miserables*. I am afraid to look up and remind myself not to be conned into searching for the summit or top ridge as they will seem deceptively close. It is still so dark. Where is the dawn?

6.20am. The first hints of sunshine in the east. From higher up, I would have probably noticed them earlier. The sunrise is muted after the rains last night. I feel tearful again, but less agitated. I realise that my Kili experience is tapping into some old wounds, especially my sense of never quite fitting in and of being left behind.

I vaguely remember saying "Jesus, I surrender", somewhere between sleeping and waking. I remember forcing myself to say the words out loud rather than just thinking them. However, I am not exactly sure what I have surrendered and how the "surrendered me" is supposed to deal with the challenges ahead.

Last night I dreamed John injured his arm and did not make it either. I hope this is just my overactive imagination rather than a premonition. I hope John is still having a good time rather than wishing he was kayaking somewhere. I hope, but I do not know. Maybe surrendering is about accepting the not-knowing rather than fighting for an illusion of control.

I am whacked again from behind, very kind as I would have fallen for some reason. I think back to the early hours when I first started to lose balance and Goody came up and interrogated me: Where was I? Where did I live? If I had failed to answer any of these questions or hesitated or stuttered, I would have been turned back, and it would have been "game over". Thank God, I am still going on up.

Steward's voice urges us on as he can now see the Stella ridge. I resolve not to get too excited as I remember from my previous trip how a ridge can tantalize and frustrate by looking closer than it is, or simply be a false ridge; once climbed, there could be another still farther ridge.

Plod, plod, plod, tick, tick, tick go my sticks. Last shot of freezing water. I hear voices above and below. The last group who left after us are behind us and another group is ahead. I imagine myself failing to reach the top due to traffic congestion.

More encouragement as we are nearly there. Someone is having difficulties, but no energy to find out who.

A bright light shines above. It is Stella!

"Come on, John", I hear people say, "or you'll miss the bus!"

I am not sure what the light is for, but I am staggering past. There is a big sign board, similar to game reserve announcements: "Stella Point Kilimanjaro Mountain Reserve."

Steward is congratulating us. The girls are congratulating me, as they thought I might drop out. I felt like it on more than one occasion, but I am here now!

The arctic flask comes round: "What drink did you order?" asks a porter.

"Ginger tea", I reply.

"No ginger here - tea or coffee only."

I sit down. My muscles are rejoicing, letting me know that my legs won't get up again. I am rooted to the rocky seat beside the path. I clutch my hot drink as Ronald parks himself by my side. Not bad. Together we are more than 120 years old.

I am not going to get up to go to Uhuru Peak though. I am shattered. There is simply nothing left. Ronald is looking shattered too. Neither of us is in the mood to go on.

I clutch my tea and wish I could stay here for a day or so. I just need rest - sleep and a meal. I should have brought a large "Leave me alone" sign, as I am "wasted" without any alcohol.

All of a sudden, it is daylight. I can now clearly see the sign at Stella, giving the height. We are on the ridge, a well-trodden crater path.

The inside of the crater looks quite different to what I remember. Perhaps my memory is confused, as I believed there was a deep crater instead of a flat floor of rock and glacier only a few hundred feet below us. The crater is covered in chalky stumps. They look like ancient walls in a ruin or Stonehenge rather than a volcano topped by a jagged lava ring like Ngorongoro.

I hear the sounds of our group moving off to *Uhuru*. "You won't get a certificate unless you go!" I hear. Gillman's, the other point on the ridge, was the furthest point our school trip got to. Only because of vague curiosity may I want to go on to the highest point Uhuru. Otherwise no regrets.

"Come on, John", I hear. Despite myself, I stagger up and move on. To my surprise, I can almost walk normally, if painfully. Sam appears and assures us that it is only a gradual mile walk to Uhuru. I don't believe him.

Sam asks a young lad to carry my rucksack. I swallow my pride, but who is going to know whether I needed it carrying like a wimp?

Now there is no order of walk. The path is gravelly and gentle, smoother than the South Downs. I watch a throng of people all heading up. Surely they have not been climbing at the same time as us. Maybe they started later and arrived just after us. The authorities should put traffic lights in.

There is also quite a flow of people coming against us. They have a "Done it!" look as they are bounding off. Will I have the same expression later?! I am envious.

"Look up, that must be Uhuru!" The object now comes clearly in sight. The group were not lying, as it is only 200 yards away.

I have told everyone of the magnificent large orange orb of an early morning sun appearing 10 times larger than normal, that I saw as a child. But when I look back east now, it may be bright with an orange to pink glow - but the sun this time shows no exceptional size and is obscured by a wall of clouds that blur the horizon.

The noise draws my attention to another timbered sign similar to the one at Stella Point - but this is possibly the most famous in Africa: "Welcome to Uhuru Point, Tanzanian Natural Reserve - highest point in Africa." A welcome sight - but surrounded by crowds of people: groups who have already been photographed and those who are waiting to be photographed by the sign.

Exhausted, I lie down. I realise that my camera is not working, so I will have to make the effort to chat to others so that I will be photographed and can prove that I have been to the top.

It is no later than eight, and the heat is rising. I am dazzled by light, and the heat is causing me to sweat so I take off the jacket lining and undershirt.

Despite the cold nights, there is no evidence of frost or snow, but the glaciers are here, dusty and layered, some now dirty looking. Someone points out that the melting of the glaciers is obvious. The layers of ice or frozen snow, which were once uniform in thickness, now show dips and bends.

I manage to ask one of the girls if she would take a couple of photos of me, which she does. I realise I will have to pose to impress. I am looking a bit staid and worn, rather than a conquering hero - in contrast to fellow-trekker Brad, who asks me to take some photos of him posing with the porters and guides. I am happy to oblige. I apply the lessons Sue taught me and take both horizontal and vertical photos, ensuring I get the glacier behind them and that his company logo shows, with porters and guides surrounding him. I try to capture the essence of the great white hunter, with the modern glam of sunglasses nonchalantly resting on his head. Then it is my turn again to be photographed in front of the Uhuru Point, waving my sticks and posing as best as I can.

It is time to head on back. The heat is on and I need a couple of hours kip at least and more than a bite to eat.

Africa is opening up brilliantly. Mount Meru to the east is clearing of fog, looking morose and stark in the light.

I am glad to get out of the hotel and reconnect with the outside world. A bit of social interaction may help me to stop brooding. John often says that I am thinking too much. My Italian and Spanish travel companions have just finished an EU conference in the hotel. They are both working on international development projects and have decided to play tourist for the day before returning to their duties.

We get caught in the morning rush hour, as our driver Haji still has to pick up our lunch. The road is full of *daladalas* that are packed with school kids and commuters.

"The cheapest transport. Never full", Haji comments. Some buses are so crowded that people's bodies hang half outside the vehicle. Each bus has an inspirational word or slogan ranging from "Hollywood", "Good Time" to "Trusting in God". I watch motorcyclists weaving in and out of the traffic.

"They are crazy people. Dangerous." Haji is clearly not a friend of those fearless men.

The traffic builds up behind large wooden crates laden with produce. Despite the pushing and pulling of several sweating men, they seem to be hardly moving. I feel sorry for these human mules. Traffic police in pristine white uniforms walk between the vehicles. How they keep their uniforms spotless in this heat and dust is beyond me. Occasionally, a vehicle gets pulled aside, but there is no other attempt to direct traffic, and so we continue to crawl along.

I have plenty of time to study the buildings on both sides of the road. Some are casually thrown together mud huts that will probably be washed away in the next rainy season. Others have been built to last. The Arusha Cultural Heritage Centre is a monument to the nation's pride in its achievements. The main building looks like a giant glass drum, a stylish fusion of tradition and modernity.

The traffic jam ends as suddenly as it has started - and is soon replaced with long stretches of road works. This means bumping along on paths without tarmac. The roads are so dry and dusty that we end up in a sandstorm every time we come near another vehicle. Haji says that the last rainy season was too short and that the rain has fallen at the wrong time. Maasai herders already have to walk many miles to feed their cows and goats. There are young boys among them, who should surely be in school.

"The Maasai do not believe in education." Haji shrugs.

We are heading back east, the sun clear and blazing, no cloud or mist now. I am glad to see the porter carrying my bag as I am nervous he will disappear with my kit. There are throngs of people around me, almost like an airport.

Back to Stella Point, we await our turn to descend. I lie down, grateful to give my legs and back a break. After a while, I am woken, and down we go. I look up wanting to recapture the moment I could first see Stella when coming up. 200 metres below, now in the sun, the rocks and sand look bland - the scenery is stark. No vegetation.

We push on down, shuffling our feet and stumbling. Each time I lurch the young porter who carries my rucksack reaches out and takes hold of me. I am grateful for the gesture, but feel embarrassed at the need for support.

I notice that our shuffling produces more sand, fine and light, good for beaches, but not for climbing. Thousands of climbers before us created this sandy path for us to struggle up, and we are contributing sand, creating hardship for those going up after us. Couldn't Summits Africa find us another route to go down to limit the ongoing damage?

Soon we are approaching the rock ledge where it was announced by Steward, on the way up, that we were more than half way there. Now we are zigzagging down, and I realise there are only a few of the original party. We have all dispersed.

There is a brilliant view of Barafu camp though some of it is obscured by the large rock outcrops. Looking back up, Stella is invisible on the crater top with its brilliant blue backing.

As I sway and stumble, the young porter is most concerned and grabs me by the hand. We trudge on, passing another stricken traveller, who is crying and rolling in the sand. His porter is trying to get him up, murmuring incentives while the climber is holding his leg and crying. What a wimp!

"Get up", I say. The sight is absurd, and I feel for the young porter trying to move the blubberer along. "Shameful", I think and then feel my porter - a lad of 18 or so - giving my hand a tug. I look up self-consciously to see if any of our group are up close and able to photograph this ensemble and post it on Facebook!

I struggle to release his grip, but he won't let go, and he does not speak English. As we push on down, Barafu approaching, I pick up the pace and keep repeating *"Hakuna Matata!"* (no worries). I also try *"Meme masuri."* (I'm alright) to reassure him, but he will not relinquish his hold. It then occurs to me that this may be an insurance issue that we are to be accompanied by porters, which explains the concern of the porter for the fallen man.

The path flattens out and I recognise the point at which we parted for the crater. No more zigzags, but straight on down, with a couple of ups!

A splash of green and orange tents greets us. At last the chance to lie down. My porter insists that we continue to the canteen tent, and finally I am free to relax on the rocks and chat with the others of the team. Of course I am one of the last down; the others have gathered outside the canteen, swapping news of the night before. I let the porter go - he is hoping for a tip, but I have no cash.

With no caffeine or food on offer I go back to the tent and strip off all cold weather clothes - long johns, jacket liners, outer socks and gloves and head covers and finally lie down. Ronald is already there, asleep.

I sleep for 20 minutes in a blissful haze as the temperature rises to the mid- twenties. As if on cue, the porters increase the tempo of conversation as they had done the previous day.

I get up and look out as the wind suddenly gets up swirling and eddying about. The chatter increases between the porter groups as I notice the tenting around the port-a-loo shaking and billowing with the wind - the loo is the centre of discussion and it sits precariously on top of a mound. As the wind increases, our tent bends and shakes, but the toilet tent billows out like a spinnaker hauled up on a mast.

The tempo of the chatter increases to accusative shouts, when with a *whoosh*, the tent breaks from its fastenings and floats high above the bare toilet and then hovers above the camp, wind filling the skirts like a hot air balloon, then tumbling down the slope in the Mwenzi direction. Shouting is now at a crescendo. The call to lunch deprives me of the finale. Most likely the groups will argue, then toss a coin and send down an unlucky lad like my previous guide to retrieve the tent.

Now cooler, I am hungry. Luckily, a larger meal is laid out. The caterers have excelled themselves with choice pieces of meat and roast potatoes.

Steward is talking about the final leg to Millennium camp, but I am engrossed with food. Everything is a delight, both smells and sight. I am tucking in and hardly notice Steward being called away by senior guides. He announces that we are to leave the meal that moment and pack up our stuff so we can go down immediately, as a storm situation is brewing. Barafu will soon be isolated by hail and snow.

Deprived of my meal, I grumpily hoist my backpack and grasp my sticks.

It takes us 2 1/2 hours to reach the Lake Manyara National Park. I am pleased to read that it belongs to the Rift Valley. John has always raved about the Rift Valley, although I am aware that he has probably never been at this particular spot, given that the valley is a mind-boggling 10,000 kilometres long!

Before we drive into the bush, there are some helpful instructions: "Remove nothing from the park except: Nourishment for the soul. Consolation for the heart. Inspiration for the mind." Nourishment - consolation - inspiration. I could do with all three. This morning my mind is stuck on the thought that after all the preparation and effort I put in, I did not get close to my desired goal. However, would I have ever felt

OK about coming down early? When would I have felt that I got value for money?

I also mull over what else a surrendered life may involve: Maybe it simply means accepting that I am not meant to play the heroine and am not cut out for "serious" adventure. I simply need to accept rather than battle my anxious nature.

It is relaxing to be driven around in a jeep and view wild animals up close - but it feels as if I am hiding in my riskless comfort zone. Surely there is more to life than being driven along by others, however pleasant the ride may be?

It is such a battle to be present in the here and now. I hope we will see the flamingos soon! There is no sign yet of the lake, whose name apparently means "wild sisal". Instead, we are surrounded by lush bush. Haji says that the park is green all year round, as it is being fed by underground waterfalls even when the main rivers dry up. Chocolate-coloured miniature lakes block the paths after yesterday's rainfall. Some grazing ground looks waterlogged. No sign of a drought here.

The dominant animals seem to be monkeys, especially baboons. We also spot the black faces of vervet monkeys. There are also so-called blue monkeys which come in many shades of grey. Haji seems disappointed that none of us is keen to take pictures. My travel companions only have their mobile phones, and I am holding out for the flamingos. I am cautious as my first camera battery ran out before I could take a picture. When I checked it in the hotel this morning, it was three quarters full. My camera obviously believes it is still up Kili!

Depending on where we drive, we are accompanied by the sounds of birds, frogs or flies. We get out of the jeep to watch some hippos. Instead of cooling down in the water, they are lying on their side, sun-bathing. I have never seen hippos in the wild so exposed, but it feels a bit like being in a giant zoo, with several tourists leaning over the safety fence to get a better view.

Later on we spot some elephants in the undergrowth, and there are giraffes grazing near Lake Manyara. At least we are told we are near the lake. All I can see are some bands of blue in the far distance. Haji says that it is not possible to get closer to the shore from here. There is not a single speck of pink anywhere. The brilliant white of egrets - yes. And the iridescent turquoise and orange of a swarm of superb starlings - but no pink.

We are on the move once again. We go south. I notice groups hurrying to Barafu from the direction we have come two days ago. I don't envy them ascending the summit in the rain. The clouds have build up and ominous sounds of thunder growl in the direction we are going.

Within a couple of hours, we reach vegetation. I can smell fir trees and enjoy the sound of birds. A clap of thunder and hail comes down. The path becomes muddy. I am slacking, as my legs are in rebellion. They feel like concrete posts. They have done enough for a month! I don't care whether we are heading up or down, as long as there is food and rest soon. I reflect that I will be closer to Sue, as we will be staying in Millennium camp. I remind myself that her mountain will have been tougher than mine. How is she feeling? What is she doing right now?

The hail, big pearly drops that strew the way, give the grey volcanic mud glitter and bling - what planet am I on? This is followed by dismal grey rain as nullifying as in Britain. Then it suddenly stops.

I am grateful that my jacket has kept me dry, although it is now at the point of letting water through. My climbing trousers have also coped well with the varied conditions.

Haji shrugs and says that it is the wrong season for flamingos. They are apparently in Arusha National Park right now, which would have been much easier (and probably cheaper!) to reach. Haji does not understand our disappointment. Has he not shown us plenty of other animals? Why bother with flamingos, which would only appear as dots on the horizon?

"But this is not what the brochure showed!" My Italian travel companion refuses to be persuaded by Haji's arguments. She is right of course.

The brochure for Lake Manyara showed flamingos in close-up skimming across the surface of the lake. The brochure gave the impression that we would be so close that we could hear the wings of the birds flapping overhead. At other times, I would have joined in the discussion and voiced my indignation about the discrepancy between the glossy advertising and reality. Today I simply take a deep breath. What is the point in arguing against reality? We need to deal with what is rather than with what could or should be.

We stop for lunch in a picnic area. The brochure would probably claim that it is directly on the shores of Lake Manyara, but once again I decide not to quibble. It is a nice view anyway. Nearby is a concrete toilet block with Western flush toilets. It is so sparkling clean, as if it has only just opened today. Now this certainly exceeds my expectations!

It is still daylight when we reach Millennium camp, sitting among the Mediterranean firs. I collapse in the tent, passing out until dinner.

I remember that it is time to tip the porters and guides. I have put the dollars I need somewhere so that they would not become damp. But where? I cannot find them anywhere. Panic sets in. I turn everything out of the backpack and empty the overnight kit bag with all the sweets and dry fruits from Samarkand. I eat some of the apricots, sour but interesting, and continue to panic.

In the early afternoon, we are heading back. Haji pulls over before we enter the road improvement section.

"Just a flat tyre", he says calmly. "No problem. Happens all the time." He tells us to stay in the jeep, but when nothing seems to be happening, we decide to get out. It looks as if we have two spare wheels, but no means of changing them! How come the carjack is so caked in mud that it cannot be operated properly if this sort of thing happens all the time? Luckily, some of Haji's buddies stop to help us out. This is what I love about Africa. Nobody is too busy to stop and chip in.

Soon we are back on the road. I am really glad Haji addressed our problem when I watch the bus in front of us race up the hill at a 45 degree angle.

"Something is wrong with that bus, Haji!"

"Yes, there is something wrong with the steering", Haji agrees, but does not seem to be too concerned.

After all, the bus driver is speeding back to Arusha to get the problem fixed!

We had planned to stop at the Arusha Snake Park on the way back, but it is too late now. I am OK with that. I have no desire to be reminded of past victories.

We run into another miniature traffic jam in Arusha, but my Spanish travel companion still reaches the hotel with 5 minutes to spare before a taxi whisks him off to the airport.

Time goes by. I can hear the clank of dishes and cutlery, but I cannot leave for fear of a porter coming in and taking the money I cannot see. Finally, at the bottom end of my sleeping bag, I find it all. Of course I put it there to be secure, as anybody can reach into a tent.

Amazingly, the first course is still out. I gobble the food down, fatigue and relief fuelling my appetite. I leave clothes out to dry overnight. I need to remember to pack them later on, but first I have to repack all the kit I have pulled out in search of the dollars, before heading to bed.

Kilimanjaro Song

"I want to be happy for everybody who made it. I want to be happy with what I have got," I keep repeating to myself. I am not sure I am there yet. I have cried every day since Monday. What if I burst into tears again and spoil everyone's sense of accomplishment? I cannot rely on my willpower to keep me composed.

I hear that another trekker had to come down the mountain just after me. Why was Greg allowed to walk all the way down, even though it took him two days? I remember a conversation between him and another trekker. He too was not feeling well on day 3. If only I had kept going for a few more hours! It is not fair. Maybe the leaders thought that I was so fragile that I would cause more problems if they did not get me off the mountain straight away. I am aware that my performance-driven mindset breeds negativity and envy, but awareness does not mean that I am now thinking differently.

The men seem to be able to get on with life in a more positive fashion. Greg says that he is happy with what he has achieved, and Grant is already planning his next Kili attempt.

I need to do something to bring this part of the journey to a positive conclusion, but I have no idea what will help. It seems right to go with Grant and Greg to welcome back the others. At least I will have a chance to see where I would have ended up if everything had gone according to plan.

We drive through banana plantations and tiny settlements where entrepreneurs are offering their wares. This part of the mountain has a more touristy feel to it. As soon as our bus stops, we are inundated with young men trying to sell their souvenirs. They do not like to take no for an answer. There is no way that I am going to stand here and listen for the next few hours to the sales pitch of the natives who want to sell me their "I climbed Kilimanjaro" ware!

We have set off so early, that it is only 10.30am when we get to the gate, and our group is not expected until lunch time...

We are up after a long lie-in and breakfast. The porter, who regularly brings the tea in the morning, comes to me while I am having breakfast and says that the porters are wanting to pull down the tents as we would be off soon. Could he collect my belongings?

Reluctantly I agree. I am suspicious as no other tents have been pulled down yet. I realise that this may be a ruse to get into my tent and steal anything of value, but I am too tired to object.

After breakfast, we have a big farewell ceremony where the porters sing the Kilimanjaro Song. The lead singer is very charismatic, jumping and leaping, arms outstretched. The other porters join the singing lustily. It is a rousing send-off. Godson makes a last speech about the mountain, and Steward reminds us that we have been the best party he has taken, with everybody supporting and encouraging the others. I am aware that I would not have made it without the support from the girls and some of the lads.

A last song in Chaga and we trek off out. The sun makes itself felt. The soil is African and red. I am relaxing on the way down as it gets warmer. I soon find a walking companion to chat to. It takes my mind off distances covered. We talk about putting the world to rights and abuse of power. I am surprised that a young person in her 20s would know about Bhopal and be aware of how many died.

We have been isolated from the world and its ways, but I am eager to get back and have a shower and sleep in a bed with sheets, not to mention have a beer!

Soon we enter the forest and can hear the chirping of forest birds and *whoosh* of colobus monkeys moving from branch to branch. Sam passes by and indicates the different flora, some small flowers only found here on the southern slopes of the mountain; there are ferns similar to ones found in wooded areas and on slopes in Britain - only these grow into palms up to twelve feet! I am too tired to pay attention.

"Do you two want to walk up the path for a bit?" I ask the men, but Grant and Greg shake their heads. They seem content to just sit and chat in the shade. Very well, I will do this alone! The path up the mountain looks too inviting. I want to walk up the hill to see what I would have seen if I had stayed with the group.

I soon find a wall to sit on. The first porters are walking past. They still have the breath for a friendly "*Jambo*", as they purposefully stride down the hill. They look as if they could easily pick up the next load and start the climb all over again. A steady stream of trekkers is walking past me. The first trekkers down the mountain are Germans. My countrymen can clearly organise more than beach towels!

Some people stop and ask me about my experience. I try to stick to the facts: "I unfortunately had to turn back at 4,198 metres, as I had problems with my blood pressure." I am aware that everyone who is walking down has worked hard and is exhausted now. They do not need to take on my emotional burden. No-one else can carry it for me anyway. Only I can unpack the load.

Some German ladies remind me that my health comes first. They are right of course. I have always said that I would not risk my life just to climb a mountain. I still wish my body had not let me down again, and part of me still feels that I have wimped out. I have to keep telling myself that my early return to the valley probably prevented serious health issues.

Altitude sickness - that verdict is still hard to swallow. Altitude sickness - too random and unpredictable for my liking. Altitude sickness - just one of many things in life that can trip us up.

A male trekker tells me that I could have taken medication for my high blood pressure. How could I if I did not know it was a problem? Why are we so often granted hindsight rather than foresight?

Before I can get bogged down again in should's, would's, could's and if only's, I remember Jesus' invitation: "Come to me, all you who are weary and burdened and I will give you rest."

I picture myself unpacking my load in front of him. I am not quite sure what I need to let go off.

"OK, Jesus, here is embarrassment."
"Keep unpacking", I sense him say.
"Regret."
"Keep going."
"That's it. There is nothing else."
"Keep going..."

"But there is nothing - oh, wait, you are right!" Digging a bit deeper, I discover that the heaviest piece of baggage is my pride. I want to be a winner but feel like a loser. I want to look good in front of others and be admired. I want to be in the limelight rather than serve backstage. I realize that I often do not appreciate journeys because I am obsessed with the destination.

"Lord, I knew this mountain would teach me valuable lessons, but I would still have preferred to learn them on the mountain top rather than at the foot of the mountain!"

A yellow butterfly is fluttering past and immediately lightens my mood. For me, butterflies are the ultimate symbol of resurrection and a changed life. I have often called myself a butterfly-in-training. A friend once pointed out that a butterfly-in-training is still a caterpillar. Maybe he is right. This week I have definitely lived like a caterpillar. Yet the butterfly reminds me that I do not have to stay the way I am.

I look down towards the gate. The voices of the sellers are only audible when I focus on them. Just as I have managed to tune out their sales pitch, I need to tune out my negative inner salesman.

Many trekkers seem to be in a reflective, pensive mood. They say that Kilimanjaro leaves no-one unchanged. It strikes me that everyone's journey will have been unique, even if they walked all the way to the summit together. Just like Greg, not all the people I see will have made it to the top, although this is what I automatically assume - just as many trekkers seem to think that I have not only been all the way up, but also got down at such lightning speed that I can now serve as their welcome committee. Well, at least I look the part of a successful trekker!

I can feel a few drops of rain, despite the sunshine. It is also getting chilly, but this time I will not turn back, even though I have left my jacket in the bus. It is 11.30am now, and there is still no sign of our group. Come on, guys! Do not let all the Germans beat you!

To distract myself, I try a word game. Can I use the letters in Kilimanjaro to write a poem which summarizes my Kili experience? Let's see. K... Knees buckling. I... Intake of breath becomes more laboured... L. laughter on the way (I wish!). I... incredible beauty (definitely true!). M... mountain-like hills. A... A... This is really hard! I do not think I am ready for poetry yet. I close my journal and start walking uphill again - *pole pole* of course. Soon the gate is out of sight. It is noon when someone calls my name.

"You recognise me?" I look at the smiling young man and shake my head.

"But I sang the Kilimanjaro Song for you all on the first day!"

"I am sorry, but I missed it. I was late for lunch. I left too early to hear any more of your songs." I am beginning to get used to listing my losses.

"OK, I will sing the song just for you." The young man looks me in the eyes and begins to sing the song that is called the "Kilimanjaro Song" over here.

"*Jambo, jambo bwana.*" I cannot help smiling at the polite exchange of greetings, followed by a randomly thrown in "Do not worry." I feel I am catching up with the others' experiences. The guide heads down and after some deliberation lets me go further up the path - as long as I promise to take it very slowly.

He is already out of sight, when I regret that I have not asked him to write down the lyrics. This would be a great song to welcome the group! I wish I had paid more attention. I have already forgotten the words beyond "*Jambo bwana*" - but, hey, those porters over there having a lunch break, they can teach me!

The porters laugh when they hear my request. One porter writes down the words in my travel journal: "*Jambo* (Hello), *Jambo bwana* (Hello sir) *Habari gani?*(How are you?) *Mzuri sana.* (I am well.) *Wageni, mwakaribishwa Kilimanjaro.* (Stranger, you are welcome here on Kilimanjaro.) *Hakuna matata.* (Do not worry)."

We take a short rest in a forest clearing. I can see a pump and transformer and know that the "world" is waiting for our return. The path is broad and has wooden planks every 3 to 4 metres to increase drainage.
The knowledge that we are "there" spurs me on - but then there are more twists and turns in the warm forest. Torment! I turn a corner and hear a familiar voice sing "*Jambo bwana*, habari yaku?"

By the time John finally runs towards me, I know the words off by heart. I knew this song would give him a new lease of life!

I can finally walk as part of the group. As long as I keep looking straight ahead, I can even pretend that I was always part of the team. All the men are sporting beards now, and some look as if they have been in a warzone. One has a scab on his nose as a reminder that he has battled both frost and scorching heat. I am relieved to see that John is not sunburned like some of the others.

When I express my longing to have shared the whole adventure, a limping Ronald says that I need to "forget the whole thing!" From the outset he has said that he would only do this kind of adventure once in his life. I predicted that he would get addicted to walking, but now I have to concede that he obviously knows his limits. He made it though, so it is easy for him to dismiss my longing to go up again - not just to stand above the horizon, but to take photos.

I flick through the photos that John has taken with my camera. There are several blurry photos of John standing on bare rocks, raising his arms in "I am the man" pose. He is wearing a T-shirt that was white before the climb. Only the ski goggles around his neck reveal that John may be a little underdressed for the weather. Then there are several pictures of the messy inside of the tent. Mmmh, not very exciting. I still remember it all too well! But, oh wait, this looks like a little chipmunk there is the corner of the tent. How cute - at least at this distance. I wouldn't have appreciated it as my tent mate.

Then a photo of the ascent. It looks as if there is a bit of a traffic jam on the way up. Climbers in high visibility jackets are trying to adjust their kit in the light of their head torches. They do not seem to pay attention to the rising sun. If I had not known better, I would have assumed that the sun was about to set, as its yellow and orange rays are being swallowed by dancing dark clouds. This photo could have been quite a stunner - if John had remembered to keep his finger off the lens! I flick to the next photo - and I am back to the beginning.

John mumbles something about the camera freezing and refusing to take further pictures. I cannot believe that there is no proper sunrise photo, nor any pictorial evidence that John made it to the top! The camera seems to be working just fine now. God, I will have to climb this mountain again one day!

Soon we are at the foot of the mountain and are greeted by Grant and Greg at the gate. They say that the park authorities did not allow them to walk up the hill without paying the appropriate fee. What fee? I didn't see anyone at the gate. I am grateful that I slipped through the net, however this happened!

Later, a mile or so, I see corrugated hut roofs, a big space for parking and many buses, trucks and traders milling about among other arrivals from the mountain.

We group together and grasp the beer bottles. Beer has never tasted so good! Down at last! After a last talk from Steward, it is good-bye to all the porters and guides we will not see at the party tonight.

What a joy to sit in comfy seats, the sun warming my fatigued thighs, as we are bumped and jostled back to the hotel for the first proper clean-up and bed in six days!

Then the hotel on the corner, the historic halfway house between Cape Town and Cairo, and our own embarkation and disembarkation point.

I am looking forward to a swim, wash and dinner in luxury, and of course a *bed*.

When I check my belongings, I notice that my wallet-like bag is missing. It contained my broken and well-used toothbrush and toothpaste. I shudder, to think that some poor soul may be brushing their teeth with my bacteria-infested toothbrush! Memo for future reference: if someone wants something from your property, they will try to rush you or make you move from familiar surroundings.

I yearn for the coast and a dip in the Indian Ocean, but in the meantime I so want to spend time with Sue. I want to know just how she has been and has coped, as my victory was entirely due to her! We have reclaimed our luggage and Sue gamely packs up. After a quick swim, it's dinner time. I eat and eat. Then we have the farewell presentation from Steward and Godson.

One by one the trekkers are called up to receive their certificates. Suddenly my name is called. Why are they calling me? I did not get far enough for one of the official certificates.

Godson hands me a photo, headed Kilimanjaro 2013. Kilimanjaro rises out of a barren landscape, both close and far at the same time. The picture must have been taken at a similar spot to where I was sent down. The picture is signed by Godson with "Well done!"

"It does not count. It does not even have the height recorded", my inner critic moans.

"O, shut up!" I tell her. "My certificate is unique. None of the official certificates have a picture of Kili."

I am pleased that Sue is presented with a certificate for climbing Kili. After all, she has gone higher than many other points in Africa.

Steward states once again that we are one of the best groups he has taken up and then we are off to celebrate. In my case it is one beer as the prices are high and the stock is low. Fatigue catches up with me. I gratefully clamber into a bed with sheets, happy that we are soon flying to Nairobi. Sue and I will be travelling down a road that holds precious memories. I never thought I would see the Athi river plains again. I am glad to be back in the valley!

A Successful Shopping Expedition

The next morning, a part of the group decides to visit the Maasai market. It is only a 10 minutes' walk from the Arusha Hotel, so the "lions" are walking alongside us as soon as we step outside the hotel. They are ignoring me today. They can sniff out the most generous "prey". Those who fall for the friendly banter of the traders are soon involved in intense sales negotiations.

However, once we reach the market, I cannot escape attention any longer. The sellers are keen to get "mama and papa" into their shops. I don't mind. I am in the mood for curio shopping.

Soon John is haggling for colourful soapstone key rings. We also buy a painting for the neighbours who have been house-sitting for us. It has the obligatory silhouette of Kilimanjaro in the background. A nice picture, but not right for me.

I am drawn to a large abstract painting that speaks of hope and love. It depicts a couple facing each other on top of a giant heart. All the colours are bold and vibrant: reds, pinks, yellows, oranges, greens and blues - there is not even a hint of grey or black.

There is just one problem. How are we going to transport it? The seller claims it will be as good as new if he rolls the canvas tightly. Even though I am not convinced, I decide to risk further disappointment.

At the local Maasai market, we have to haggle and barter for everything. It is tiring to be back in the "world", but at least I return with a new toothbrush - proof that you can buy anything in an African market!

Epilogue

Almost a year to the day after conquering Kili, I was struck with deep vein thrombosis - a jolt out of the blue, as the usual reasons for getting it did not apply in my case. Blood tests have revealed that I have Leiden V, a genetic condition that increases the risk of blood clots. Although I have recovered, a line has been drawn.

For the first time, it has occurred to me that I can no longer do what I want. It is not simply a case of being slower in the race, but no longer being able to go where I went before. No more high altitudes and long haul flights for me. So farewell, Africa; *kwaheri*, Kilimanjaro - it was an unforgettable adventure.

I now feel reconciled with the land of my birth. I saw hope and a growing awareness of one's neighbour.

I would not have found closure if Sue had not developed a passion for Africa. It was Sue's persistence, eye for detail and organisation that ensured my climbing success - this expedition was truly a team effort.

I now have many precious memories, like plodding up to Lava Tower, the struggle to the summit and the camaraderie with fellow trekkers and our guides. However far back it already seems, I will cherish the knowledge that I was on the Roof of Africa for a while. Now I must face the foothills.

Even though nothing compares so far with the euphoria of conquering Kili again, I hope that life will still contain some mountain-top experiences.

A week after the climb, my blood pressure was back to normal and my pulse rate in the 70s. When we got home, I went straight back to the gym. Fitness is for life, not just for Kili after all. I currently have more energy than I have had for most of my adult life.

In hindsight, it would have been better if I had waited until my health issues were fully resolved before attempting the climb, but I am aware that a better timing for me would have been the wrong timing for John. Given his blood disorder, it is a miracle that he managed to climb Kilimanjaro twice.

My resolve never to bake another flapjack did not last long - the smell and taste of freshly baked flapjacks is simply too appealing. However, I am learning to carry less provisions when I am travelling.

When I unrolled the souvenir picture, the paint had cracked and peeled in several places. I painted over the cracks with crayons and watercolours. When you look closely, you can tell where I took over from the original artist, but that seems apt. Life is messy and imperfect.

The disappointment of not making it to the top is no longer a gaping, sore wound, but a scar that can still be sensitive to the touch. Some things are unresolved and may remain so. Were my problems caused by altitude sickness or the wrong medical treatment before I started the climb? I will never know for sure, just as I will never know why John and I were not able to have children.

We can still have "babies" of course, projects John and I can both add value to. I consider this book our firstborn.

I have realised that the most challenging mountains are the ones inside. There was a mountain I *wanted* to climb, but there is a mountain range I *need* to climb. Pride, doubt, grief - these mountains are more formidable than any physical mountain I could ever scale. No, I am not expecting to get to the top any time soon - some mountains take a lifetime to climb.

Printed in Great Britain
by Amazon